Atmosphere and Weather

Connecting Students to Science Series

By
LaVerne Logan and Don Powers, Ph.D.

COPYRIGHT © 2002 Mark Twain Media, Inc.

ISBN 1-58037-218-X

Printing No. CD-1564

Mark Twain Media, Inc., Publishers
Distributed by Carson-Dellosa Publishing Company, Inc.

Table of Contents

Introduction to the Series

The Connecting Students to Science Series is designed for grades 5–8. This series will introduce the following topics: Simple Machines, Electricity and Magnetism, Rocks and Minerals, Atmosphere and Weather, and Chemistry. Each book will contain an introduction to the topic, naive concepts, inquiry activities, content integration, children's literature connections, curriculum resources, assessment documents, a bibliography, and materials lists. Students will develop an understanding of the concepts and processes of science through the use of good scientific techniques. Students will be engaged in higher-level thinking skills while doing fun and interesting activities. All of the activities will be aligned with the National Science Education Standards (NSES) and National Council of Teachers of Mathematics (NCTM) Standards.

This series is written for classroom teachers, parents, families, and students. The books in this series can be used as a full unit of study or as individual lessons to supplement existing textbooks or curriculum programs. Activities are designed to be pedagogically sound, hands-on, minds-on science activities that support the NSES. Parents and students could use this series as an enhancement to what is being done in the classroom or as a tutorial at home. The procedures and content background are clearly explained in the introduction and within the individual activities. Materials used in the activities are commonly found in classrooms and homes.

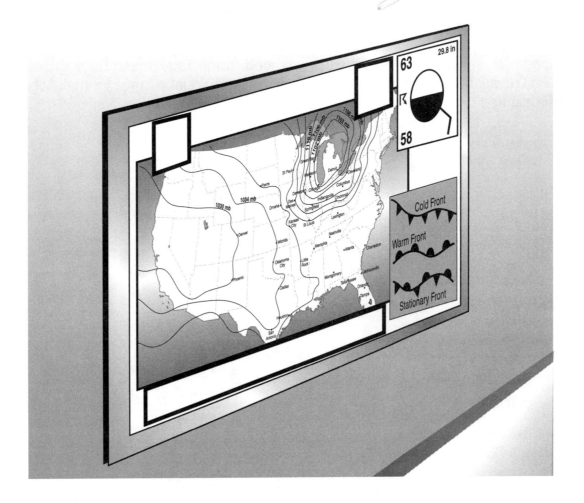

Introduction to the Topic and Major Concepts

Weather impacts what we wear, how we move, our economy, our health, our daily activities, and in short, nearly every aspect of human activity. Yet, students may take weather for granted, as it is all around them all the time. The activities in this book are designed to cause students to pause and think critically about weather and its influence on humans.

The study of weather provides many opportunities to examine the interaction of physical science principles within the context of earth science. In addition to the observable elements of weather, such as rain, snow, clouds, lightning, rainbows, etc., it is important to consider less observable concepts, e.g., latent heat, dew point, temperature, humidity.

Initially, students may readily consider weather on a horizontal basis, that is, weather on the earth's surface. While this is important, the vertical aspect of weather should be reinforced as well. Throughout the activities in this book, students may observe, predict, collect and record data, make inferences, and create models. Students are asked to think in an inquiry mode. It is strongly recommended that teachers and parents provide students with ongoing opportunities to examine and challenge their current understandings, pose their own questions, and seek answers.

The activities in this book are designed to provide starting points for this manner of teaching and learning. The Procedures section of each activity is directed toward the teacher or parent as a guide to setting up the activity. The Summary/What to Look For section is also a teacher/parent section that can be used to determine how well the student has mastered the concepts.

Space for student free response is provided in the Exploration/Data Collection and Discussion Questions/Assessment sections; however, individual science journals/logs may be readily substituted.

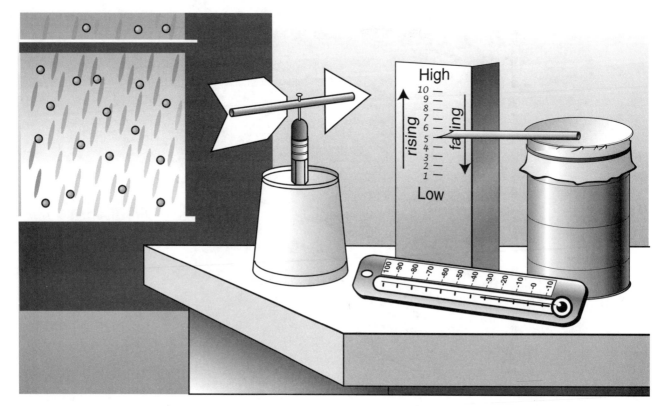

Naive Concepts and Terminology Definitions

Introduction: Our understanding of the natural world is directly related to everyday experience, including experiences in and out of the science classroom. Sometimes the everyday descriptions of phenomena lead to concepts that are either incomplete or inaccurate. For example, we may observe a glass of iced tea with water collecting and running down the outside of the glass and state, "The glass is sweating." Such a statement may lead us to inaccurately infer as to the source of the moisture on the outside of the glass. A careful and thoughtful analysis of this phenomena might lead us to infer that the moisture on the outside of the glass is condensation and that the source of the moisture is the water vapor from the surrounding air. We may refer to our developing conception of the world and the way things work or the way life works as being in the process of development. In this way, some of our ideas may be naive. Some authors prefer referring to these developing concepts as misconceptions; however, we will refer to them as naive ideas.

Some Naive Ideas Related to Weather:

One area for potential naive conceptions is related to the terminology used. Many commonly-used words have a specific and alternative meaning in science. A second area that may serve as a source for naive conceptions occurs when intuitive ideas gained through everyday experiences are contrary to the more formal structure of scientific concepts.

Words that may serve as a source for confusion include:

- **advection** - the horizontal movement of weather phenomena, such as warmth and humidity. Students may focus on weather conditions and phenomena at the earth's surface; whereas, they should also consider a vertical perspective as well.

- **air pressure** - a measurement of force, exerted on a given unit of space, by the weight of air; measured in kilopascals and reported in millibars (mb) and/or inches of mercury. Also known as barometric pressure. Students may wrongly assume barometric pressure is uniform throughout the earth's surface (14.7 pounds per square inch at sea level).

- **angle of incidence** - the angle at which the sun's rays strike the earth's surface.

- **angle of reflection** - the angle at which the sun's rays bounce off the surface of the earth. The proportion of the sun's energy that is reflected off is known as **albedo**. Students may wrongly assume all areas of the earth have the same albedo.

- **atmosphere** - the air that surrounds the earth; the majority of our weather data is taken from the troposphere, the layer of the atmosphere closest to the earth, which extends up seven to eight miles.

- **cloud droplets** - tiny drops of water that form as water condenses, thereby forming clouds. Students may confuse cloud droplets (0.02 mm diameter) and raindrops (0.5 mm in diameter).

- **condensation** - a physical phase change from the property of gaseous matter to liquid matter.

Naive Concepts and Terminology Definitions (cont.)

- **condensation nuclei** - tiny particles (e.g., smoke and dust) around which cloud droplets form; students may consider cloud droplets as water vapor; whereas, water vapor is invisible.

- **Coriolis Effect** - deflection of winds caused by the rotation of the earth on its axis.

- **dew point** - a measure of humidity in the air (e.g., the temperature at which dew will begin forming). Condensation occurs assuming constant pressure. Students may confuse *temperature* and *dew point.*

- **evaporation** - a physical phase change from the property of liquid matter to gaseous matter.

- **fog** - a cloud that forms at the surface of the earth. Students may not associate fog as a cloud, perhaps because of its location.

- **heat** - students may confuse the terms *heat* and *temperature;* heat refers to a form of energy that flows from one object to a cooler object. Equal amounts of heat applied to two objects will not necessarily result in the same temperature differences; it depends upon the material.

- **humidity** - the moisture in the air.

- **hurricane** - a tropical cyclone with wind speeds of at least 74 mph or more.

- **insolation** - the radiant energy from the sun received by the earth; students may confuse this term with *insulation.*

- **isobars** - lines on a weather map that connect areas of equal barometric pressure.

- **isotherms** - lines on a weather map that connect areas of equal temperature.

- **latent heat** - energy stored when evaporation turns a liquid into a gas and is later released when condensation occurs.

- **relative humidity** - the amount of moisture in a given amount of air relative to what could be contained if the given amount of air were completely saturated; measured and reported as a percentage.

- **temperature** - temperature is the average kinetic energy (of particles) of an object; students may confuse the terms *temperature* and *heat.*

- **water cycle** - also known as the hydrologic cycle; the exchange of water between land, bodies of water, and the atmosphere.

- **water vapor** - water in a gaseous state; students may confuse clouds and water vapor; whereas, water vapor is invisible.

National Standards

***National Science Education Standards (NSES) Content Standards* (NRC, 1996)**
National Research Council (1996). *National Science Education Standards.* Washington, D.C.:
    National Academy Press.

Unifying Concepts K-12
Systems, Order, and Organization - The natural and designed world is complex. Scientists and students learn to define small portions for the convenience of investigation. The units of investigation can be referred to as systems. A **system** is an organized group of related objects or components that form a whole. Systems can consist of machines.

Systems, Order, and Organization

The goal of this standard is to …
• Think and analyze in terms of systems.
• Assume that the behavior of the universe is not capricious. Nature is predictable.
• Understand the regularities in a system.
• Understand that prediction is the use of knowledge to identify and explain observations.
• Understand that the behavior of matter, objects, organisms, or events has order and can be described statistically.

Evidence, Models, and Explanation

The goal of this standard is to …
• Recognize that evidence consists of observations and data on which to base scientific explanations.
• Recognize that models have explanatory power.
• Recognize that scientific explanations incorporate existing scientific knowledge (laws, principles, theories, paradigms, models) and new evidence from observations, experiments, or models.
• Recognize that scientific explanations should reflect a rich scientific knowledge base, evidence of logic, higher levels of analysis, greater tolerance of criticism and uncertainty, and a clear demonstration of the relationship between logic, evidence, and current knowledge.

Change, Constancy, and Measurement

The goal of this standard is to …
• Recognize that some properties of objects are characterized by constancy, including the speed of light, the charge of an electron, and the total mass plus energy of the universe.
• Recognize that changes might occur in the properties of materials, position of objects, motion, and form and function of systems.
• Recognize that changes in systems can be quantified.
• Recognize that measurement systems may be used to clarify observations.

National Standards (cont.)

Form and Function

The goal of this standard is to …

- Recognize that the form of an object is frequently related to its use, operation, or function.
- Recognize that function frequently relies on form.
- Recognize that form and function apply to different levels of organization.
- Enable students to explain function by referring to form and explain form by referring to function.

NSES Content Standard A: Inquiry

- Abilities necessary to do scientific inquiry
  - Identify questions that can be answered through scientific investigations.
  - Design and conduct a scientific investigation.
  - Use appropriate tools and techniques to gather, analyze, and interpret data.
  - Develop descriptions, explanations, predictions, and models using evidence.
  - Think critically and logically to make relationships between evidence and explanations.
  - Recognize and analyze alternative explanations and predictions.
  - Communicate scientific procedures and explanations.
  - Use mathematics in all aspects of scientific inquiry.
- Understanding about inquiry
  - Different kinds of questions suggest different kinds of scientific investigations.
  - Current scientific knowledge and understanding guide scientific investigations.
  - Mathematics is important in all aspects of scientific inquiry.
  - Technology used to gather data enhances accuracy and allows scientists to analyze and quantify results of investigations.
  - Scientific explanations emphasize evidence, have logically consistent arguments, and use scientific principles, models, and theories.
  - Science advances through legitimate skepticism.
  - Scientific investigations sometimes result in new ideas and phenomena for study, generate new methods or procedures, or develop new technologies to improve data collection.

NSES Content Standard B: Properties and Changes of Properties in Matter 5–8

NSES Content Standard D: Structure of the Earth System 5–8

NSES Content Standard D: Earth in the Solar System 5–8

NSES Content Standard E: Science and Technology 5–8

- Abilities of technological design
  - Identify appropriate problems for technological design.
  - Design a solution or product.
  - Implement the proposed design.
  - Evaluate completed technological designs or products.
  - Communicate the process of technological design.

National Standards (cont.)

- Understanding about science and technology
  - Scientific inquiry and technological design have similarities and differences.
  - Many people in different cultures have made and continue to make contributions.
  - Science and technology are reciprocal.
  - Perfectly designed solutions do not exist.
  - Technological designs have constraints.
  - Technological solutions have intended benefits and unintended consequences.

NSES Content Standard F: Science in Personal and Social Perspectives 5–8
- Science and technology in society
  - Science influences society through its knowledge and world view.
  - Societal challenges often inspire questions for scientific research.
  - Technology influences society through its products and processes.
  - Scientists and engineers work in many different settings.
  - Science cannot answer all questions, and technology cannot solve all human problems.

NSES Content Standard G: History and Nature of Science 5–8
- Science as a human endeavor
- Nature of science
  - Scientists formulate and test their explanations of nature using observation, experiments, and theoretical and mathematical models.
  - It is normal for scientists to differ with one another about interpretation of evidence and theory.
  - It is part of scientific inquiry for scientists to evaluate the results of other scientists' work.
- History of science
  - Many individuals have contributed to the traditions of science.
  - Science has been and is practiced by different individuals in different cultures.
  - Tracing the history of science can show how difficult it was for scientific innovators to break through the accepted ideas of their time to reach the conclusions we now accept.

National Standards (cont.)

Standards for Technological Literacy (STL) International Technology Education Association (2000)
International Technology Education Association (2000). *Standards for Technological Literacy.* Reston, VA: International Technology Education Association.

The Nature of Technology
Students will develop an understanding of the …
1. Characteristics and scope of technology.
2. Core concepts of technology.
3. Relationships among technologies and the connections between technology and other fields of study.

Technology and Society
Students will develop an understanding of the …
4. Cultural, social, economic, and political effects of technology.
5. Effects of technology on the environment.
6. Role of society in the development and use of technology.
7. Influence of technology on history.

Design
Students will develop an understanding of the …
8. Attributes of design.
9. Engineering design.
10. Role of troubleshooting, research and development, invention and innovation, and experimentation in problem solving.

Abilities for a Technological World
Students will develop abilities to …
11. Apply the design process.
12. Use and maintain technological products and systems.
13. Assess the impact of products and systems.

The Designed World
Students will develop an understanding of and be able to select and use …
14. Medical technologies.
15. Agricultural and related biotechnologies.
16. Energy and power technologies.
17. Information and communication technologies.
18. Transportation technologies.
19. Manufacturing technologies.
20. Construction technologies.

National Standards (cont.)

Principles and Standards for School Mathematics (NCTM, 2000)
National Council for Teachers of Mathematics (2000). *Principles and Standards for School Mathematics.* Reston, VA: National Council for Teachers of Mathematics.

Numbers and Operations
Students will be enabled to …
- Understand numbers, ways of representing numbers, relationships among numbers, and number systems.
- Understand the meanings of operations and how they relate to one another.
- Compute fluently and make reasonable estimates.

Algebra
Students will be enabled to …
- Understand patterns, relations, and functions.
- Represent and analyze mathematical situations and structures using algebraic symbols.
- Use mathematical models to represent and understand quantitative relationships.
- Analyze change in various contexts.

Geometry
Students will be enabled to …
- Analyze characteristics and properties of two- and three-dimensional geometric shapes and develop mathematical arguments about geometric relationships.
- Specify locations and describe spatial relationships using coordinate geometry and other representational systems.
- Apply transformations and use symmetry to analyze mathematical situations.
- Use visualization, spatial reasoning, and geometric modeling to solve problems.

Measurement
Students will be enabled to …
- Understand measurable attributes of objects and the units, systems, and processes of measurement.
- Apply appropriate techniques, tools, and formulas to determine measurements.

Data Analysis and Probability
Students will be enabled to …
- Formulate questions that can be addressed with data and collect, organize, and display relevant data to answer them.
- Select and use appropriate statistical methods to analyze data.
- Develop and evaluate inferences and predictions that are based on data.
- Understand and apply basic concepts of probability.

Science Process Skills

Introduction: Science is organized curiosity, and an important part of this organization is the thinking skills or information processing skills. We ask the question "Why?" and then must plan a strategy for answering. In the process of answering our questions, we make and carefully record observations, make predictions, identify and control variables, measure, make inferences, and communicate our findings. Additional skills may be called upon depending upon the nature of our questions. In this way, science is a verb involving active manipulation of materials and careful thinking. Science is dependent upon language, math, and reading skills, as well as the specialized thinking skills associated with identifying and solving problems.

BASIC PROCESS SKILLS:

Classifying: Grouping, ordering, arranging, or distributing objects, events, or information into categories based on properties or criteria, according to some method or system.

> Example—Classifying cloud types, snowflakes, forms of precipitation

Observing: Using the senses (or extensions of the senses) to gather information about an object or event.

> Example—Observing wind direction, cloud formation, whether it is sunny or cloudy, whether it is raining or clear

Measuring: Using both standard and nonstandard measures or estimates to describe the dimensions of an object or event; making quantitative observations.

> Example—Measuring temperature, measuring the amount of precipitation, measuring wind speed and direction, measuring relative humidity

Inferring: Making an interpretation or conclusion based on reasoning to explain an observation.

> Example—Stating that because barometric pressure is falling rapidly, a storm is coming

Communicating: Communicating ideas through speaking or writing. Students may share the results of investigations, collaborate on solving problems, and gather and interpret data, both orally and in writing. Using graphs, charts, and diagrams to describe data.

> Example—Describing an event or a set of observations. Participating in brainstorming and hypothesizing before an investigation. Formulating initial and follow-up questions in the study of a topic. Summarizing data, interpreting findings, and offering conclusions. Questioning or refuting previous findings. Making decisions. Use of a map to show the locations of high- and low-pressure systems. Use of weather symbols common to meteorology.

Science Process Skills (cont.)

Predicting: Making a forecast of future events or conditions in the context of previous observations and experiences.

> Example—Stating, "Based on previous data, the climate is gradually warming."

Manipulating Materials: Handling or treating materials and equipment skillfully and effectively.

> Example—Using a wind vane to measure wind direction. Using a thermometer to measure temperature. Using a barometer to measure barometric pressure.

Using Numbers: Applying mathematical rules or formulas to calculate quantities or to determine relationships from basic measurements.

> Example—Measuring and charting temperature, wind speed and direction, relative humidity, and barometric pressure.

Developing Vocabulary: Specialized terminology and unique uses of common words in relation to a given topic need to be identified and given meaning.

> Example—Using context clues, working definitions, glossaries or dictionaries, word structure (roots, prefixes, suffixes), and synonyms and antonyms to clarify meaning (i.e., cirrus, stratus, cumulus, altostratus, alto cumulus, cumulonimbus).

Questioning: Questions serve to focus inquiry, determine prior knowledge, and establish purposes or expectations for an investigation. An active search for information is promoted when questions are used.

> Example—Using what is already known about a topic or concept to formulate questions for further investigation, hypothesizing and predicting prior to gathering data, or formulating questions as new information is acquired.

Using Cues: Key words and symbols convey significant meaning in messages. Organizational patterns facilitate comprehension of major ideas. Graphic features clarify textual information.

> Example—Listing or underlining words and phrases that carry the most important details, or relating key words together to express a main idea or concept.

INTEGRATED PROCESS SKILLS:

Creating Models: Displaying information by means of graphic illustrations or other multisensory representations.

> Example—Drawing a graph or diagram, constructing a three-dimensional object, using a digital camera to record an event, constructing a chart or table, or producing a picture or map that illustrates information about current or future weather.

Science Process Skills (cont.)

Formulating Hypotheses: Stating or constructing a statement that is testable about what is thought to be the expected outcome of an experiment (based on reasoning).

> Example—Making a statement to be used as the basis for an experiment: "If the barometric pressure changes, a change in the weather will occur."

Generalizing: Drawing general conclusions from particulars.

> Example—Making a summary statement following the analysis of experimental results: "The overall temperature of an area increases as the rays of the sun strike the area at a more direct angle."

Identifying and Controlling Variables: Recognizing the characteristics of objects or factors in events that are constant or change under different conditions and that can affect an experimental outcome, keeping most variables constant while manipulating only one variable.

> Example—Taking and recording weather readings at the same time of day and in the same location.

Defining Operationally: Stating how to measure a variable in an experiment; defining a variable according to the actions or operations to be performed on or with it.

> Example—Defining snowfall as the average of five different measurements of snowfall.

Recording and Interpreting Data: Collecting bits of information about objects and events that illustrate a specific situation; organizing and analyzing data that has been obtained and drawing conclusions from it by determining apparent patterns or relationships in the data.

> Example—Recording data (taking notes, making lists/outlines, recording numbers on charts/graphs, making tape recordings, taking photographs, writing numbers of results of observations/measurements) from observations to determine an overall view of the current weather conditions.

Making Decisions: Identifying alternatives and choosing a course of action from among alternatives after basing the judgment for the selection on justifiable reasons.

> Example—Determining optimum location(s) for weather data collecting station(s).

Experimenting: Being able to conduct an experiment, including asking an appropriate question, stating a hypothesis, identifying and controlling variables, operationally defining those variables, designing a "fair" experiment, and interpreting the results of an experiment.

> Example—Formulating a researchable question, identifying and controlling variables, including a manipulated and responding variable, data collection, data analysis, drawing conclusions, and formulating new questions as a result of the conclusions.

Name: _____ Date: _____

Student Inquiry Activity **1**: Angle of Incidence

Topic: Weather—Sun's Rays

Introductory Statement:

The sun plays an important role in our daily weather, seasons, and climate. In these activities, you will observe the effects of the angle at which the sun strikes the earth on our weather.

NSES Content Standards D: Earth in the Solar System

The sun is the major source of energy for phenomena on the earth's surface, such as the growth of plants, winds, ocean currents, and the water cycle. Seasons result from variations in the amount of the sun's energy hitting the surface, due to the tilt of the earth's rotation on its axis and the length of the day.

Science Skills and Concepts:

- Students will infer the relationship between the angle of incidence and the temperature.
- Students will observe the angle of incidence of the sun's radiant energy.
- Students will record the causes of Earth's weather.
- Students will analyze a model of the sun's radiant energy.

Materials/Safety Concerns:

three light sources (flexible lamps, 150-watt bulbs)	three thermometers
timing device	student data recording sheet
one flashlight for each group of students	large sheets of white freezer paper
one basketball or globe for each group of students	markers

Content Background:

The sun and its interaction with the earth's atmosphere is the driving force for our weather. Students may associate the sun with heat and warm temperatures, but it is also responsible for weather phenomena, such as blizzards, tornadoes, hurricanes, winds, clouds, fronts, and rainstorms. The focus of this lesson is on the effects of the angle of incoming solar radiant energy on temperature. A key concept is the **angle of incidence**, or the angle at which the sun's rays strike the earth. Students will observe several models that demonstrate a relationship between the angle of the sun's rays and the intensity of energy. This concept illustrates the uneven heating of the earth's surface, the catalyst for much of our weather. Although sources vary, roughly half of the incoming solar energy is absorbed by the earth's surface while roughly half is absorbed by the atmosphere or reflected back into space (Sager, et. al., 2002; Williams, 1997; Graedel and Crutzen, 1995). Emphasis of the models in this lesson is on the percentage of solar radiation that reaches the earth's surface, particularly angles of incidence and resultant temperatures. Weather-related concepts such as day/night and seasons can easily be interjected, as the tilt, rotation, and revolution of the earth may also be considered within the models.

Name: _____   Date: _____

Student Inquiry Activity **1** : Angle of Incidence (cont.)

Procedures:

1. Encourage students to write down what they believe to be the cause(s) of weather. They will likely write about specific weather events. Examine their writing for evidence of the role of the sun in weather.

2. Arrange three light sources at angles so they all shine on thermometers from (1) directly overhead, (2) 45 degrees, and (3) 90 degrees. Be sure that the distance between the lamp and the thermometers is equal.

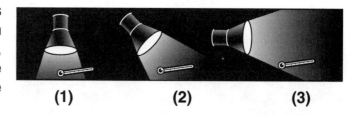

(1)   **(2)**   **(3)**

Have students predict if the temperatures will vary over time; have them include a supporting rationale for their thinking. Record any differences in temperature over a one-hour period, e.g., every 15 minutes. Have students explain the results using the data collected, (temperatures). Discuss the implications for our weather.

3. Arrange students into groups of two or three. Provide a large sheet of white freezer paper and one flashlight per group. This activity works best if the room is darkened. Instruct students to lay the paper flat on a table. Measure a height of 50 centimeters. From this height, students should shine the light directly onto the paper (e.g., lens of flashlight should be parallel to the tabletop). Have one student trace and label the outline of the light pattern from this angle. Next, while holding the distance constant, rotate the flashlight 45 degrees to one side. Again, have students trace and label the outline of the light pattern. Lastly, rotate the flashlight to 10 degrees (again, keeping the distance constant), and have students trace and label the outline of the light pattern.

90°   **45°**   **10°**

Have students calculate the area of each of the three patterns; estimate in square centimeters if necessary. Compare by posting or displaying the outline drawings within groups; determine variance and what factors may have caused this.

4. Provide each group of students with a basketball or globe. Using the basketball or globe as a model of the earth, have a student hold the flashlight 10 cm away from the equator with the rays striking the "equator-line" directly; observe and record the path of the rays (on paper). Have students observe and record (on paper) the path of the rays, as before. Holding the light steady, raise it straight up so that the light shines roughly on the latitudes of the United States (hold the ball still for now, but check to make sure students recognize that the earth rotates and revolves; explain that for the purposes of this activity, a freeze-frame demonstration is being used). Move the flashlight up to the poles and observe and record (on paper) the path of the rays, once again. Question students about the implications of the angle of incidence in relation to the various movements of the earth (rotation and revolution; the tilt of the earth).

Name: _____ Date: _____

Student Inquiry Activity **1** : Angle of Incidence (cont.)

5. Discuss in what ways the angle of incidence affects the surface area coverage. Ask students to predict the effects of the angle of incidence on temperature. Check to see if students recognize that the same amount of energy is being spread out over a greater surface area. Using all three demonstrations, ask students to draw parallels to the earth's incoming radiant energy and the effects on weather.

_ _

Exploration/Data Collection:

What Causes Our Weather?

Part 1—Lamp and Thermometer Demonstration

Overhead   **45°**   **90°**

1. My prediction(s) regarding the temperatures are _____

    _____

    _____

    _____

2. I think this because _____

    _____

    _____

    _____

Part 2—Flashlight and Paper

90°   **45°**   **10°**

1. Observe and record the area of the light pattern for each of the following positions:

    Directly Overhead (50 cm)   45 degrees (50 cm)   10 degrees (50 cm)

    _____   _____   _____

Name: _____ Date: _____

Student Inquiry Activity 1 : Angle of Incidence (cont.)

2. Observations that I have made. _____

_____

_____

_____

Part 3—Flashlight and Basketball

1. Pretend that the flashlight represents the sun and the basketball represents the earth. Observe and record drawings of the "sun's rays" for each of the following positions:

directly at the side of the ball	at "North America"	at the "North Pole"

2. Carefully observe the point at which the "sun's rays" strike the "earth" in each of the drawings above. Add angles to each drawing by asking yourself … "If the sun's rays bounced off the surface of the earth, in which direction would they most likely go?"

Summary/What to Look For:

1. To what extent were students' original ideas of the causes of weather altered?
2. To what extent were students able to infer the relationship between the angle of incidence and temperature?
3. To what extent were students able to synthesize the angle of incidence and the movements of the earth? The tilt of the earth?

Discussion Questions/Assessment

1. T or F   The earth is not always the same distance from the sun during the year. Explain your reasoning.

_____

_____

_____

Name: _____   Date: _____

Student Inquiry Activity **1**: Angle of Incidence (cont.)

2. T or F   The Midwest experiences the highest temperatures when the earth is the closest to the sun during the year. Explain your reasoning.

_____

_____

_____

3. T or F   The sun's rays all travel the same distance to reach the earth.

_____

_____

_____

4. In what ways would our weather be affected if the earth were not tilted?

_____

_____

_____

5. In what ways would our weather and world be affected if the earth did not rotate?

_____

_____

_____

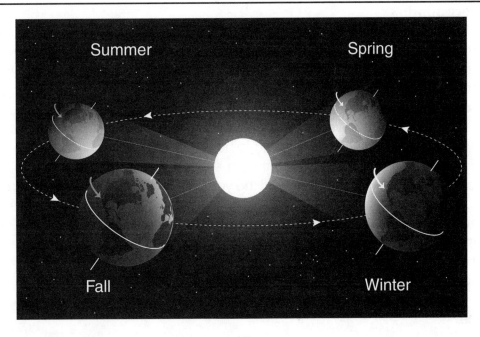

Student Inquiry Activity **2**: Heating of Earth's Atmosphere/ Surface

Topic: Weather—Heat Absorption

Introductory Statement:

In this activity, you will test to determine factors that influence what happens to the sun's radiant energy as it strikes the earth.

> **NSES Content Standards D: Earth in the Solar System**
>
> The sun is the major source of energy for phenomena on the earth's surface, such as the growth of plants, winds, ocean currents, and the water cycle. Seasons result from variations in the amount of the sun's energy hitting the surface, due to the tilt of the earth's rotation on its axis and the length of the day.

Science Skills and Concepts:

- Students will hypothesize and test the relationship between surface color and heat absorption.
- Students will hypothesize and test the relationship between surface texture and heat absorption.
- Students will infer how the color and texture of earth materials impact the temperature when exposed to sunlight.

Materials/Safety Concerns:

various colors of construction paper   scissors
tape   stapler
thermometers   light sources/lamps
If indoors, containers of sand, gravel, water, grass clippings, soil
Note: Students should be closely monitored if working around larger bodies of water, large piles of sand, gravel, etc.

Content Background:

As we have discovered earlier, the sun's radiant energy is vitally important to our survival on Earth. Without it, we would no longer exist. The sun's radiant energy is directly responsible for driving the earth's weather. The heating and cooling of the earth and its atmosphere is inherent within weather and climate. This process is analogous to a heat engine (Williams, 1997), which drives an energy budget; whereby, heat gain and loss must be balanced within the context of weather and climate. Water heats and cools more slowly than rocks, sand, and soils. Students may recall a beach where the sand is hot during the day and cooler in the evening; whereas, the water remains warmer well into the evening. How do these principles affect our weather? Polar water remains cold throughout the year, while tropical water retains large amounts of heat throughout the year, despite the effects of seasons. The polar and tropical waters and their temperatures directly affect the earth's atmosphere. Temperatures in land regions, on the other hand, are much more influenced by the earth's seasons. The interface between air warmed and cooled by tropical and polar waters and air over land regions is a critical element to understanding our weather. This lesson examines the effects of the sun's rays as they strike various parts of the earth's surface, specifically with respect to physical characteristics of the earth's surface.

Name: _____ Date: _____

Student Inquiry Activity 2 : Heating of Earth's Atmosphere/ Surface (cont.)

Procedures:

1. Clarify the definition of temperature as a measure of heat. Poll the class regarding the influence of temperature within the context of weather. Ask students to share weather-related experiences in which they have noticed differences in temperature. What factors appear to influence the temperature? In most cases, the time of year (season) will emerge as a primary cause of temperature variation. Using this discussion, review the content gained from the first activity (Angle of Incidence). Point out that this activity will build on these understandings as the students further examine the sun's rays as they strike the earth, particularly as surfaces vary, e.g., soil, water, rocks, grass, etc.

2. Arrange students into groups of your choice. This activity consists of two parts, each of which requires a small amount of set-up time and extended periods of data recording. Both allow for other activities to be done as long as data collection opportunities are provided anywhere from every 15 minutes to every hour. Both activities can be simulated inside, but outside set-up is preferable.

Part One:

1. Review the discussion to see if color was mentioned as a contributing factor to temperature. In groups of three or four, instruct students to construct small pockets (similar to a library card pocket inside a book) made of construction paper. Vary the color of each pocket; black, white, brown, green, yellow, etc.

2. Insert a thermometer into the open end of each pocket. Tape the top of the pocket closed with the thermometer still inside, while allowing the thermometer to be slipped out to be read.

3. Predict what will happen to the temperature in each of the pockets if they are all placed in direct view of the sun (or lamp) at the same angle. Note … be sure to encourage students to control all variables, although an extension may be to vary angle, location, elevation, etc.

4. After variables have been identified and controlled, place the thermometers outside within direct view of the sun (or lamp). Record temperatures at 15-minute intervals for a period of one hour (longer if possible).

Name: _____ Date: _____

Student Inquiry Activity 2 : Heating of Earth's Atmosphere/ Surface (cont.)

Part Two:

1. Students will investigate the effects of various earth substances and textures on temperature. Encourage students to design controlled investigations to determine how various common earth substances (sand, soil, water, rocks, grass, etc.) react to sunlight (e.g., In what way(s) is temperature affected?). This activity requires

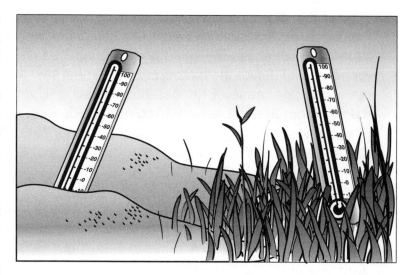

additional time as some substances will require longer periods of time to absorb heat. Students may wish to track temperature changes throughout the day. Depending on the location, implant thermometers within each medium so the area is clearly marked and the thermometers can be read periodically. Large containers/areas of each medium are preferable (e.g., ponds or a large tank, large sand piles, gravel pile). Have students record temperatures every 15 minutes to one hour throughout the day. Have students record observations that they believe to be an influence on the outcome(s) of the investigation. Other variables to be considered are the depth of the thermometer, moisture content, cloud cover, etc.

Extension: Students may also experience the opposite effect (cooling rates) if the activity can be conducted at home after the sun has gone down.

3. After adequate data has been recorded and analyzed, discuss the findings as a large group. Provide students an opportunity to communicate and compare their findings, especially if different independent variables were examined. Discuss any parallels between inferences and conclusions drawn from Parts 1 and 2.

Management Tip: For teachers in departmentalized settings, perhaps this activity could be started by one class and checked periodically by students from subsequent classes throughout the day.

Name: _____ Date: _____

Student Inquiry Activity 2: Heating of Earth's Atmosphere/Surface (cont.)

Exploration/Data Collection:

What Difference Does It Make?

Part 1 - Does Color Make a Difference?

1. Predict how the color of a surface will impact the temperature when exposed to sunlight.

    _____

    _____

    _____

2. My reasons for thinking this are _____

    _____

    _____

    _____

3. Use the chart below (or create your own) to collect and record temperatures. Create a line graph to track changes over time.

Data Collection Chart

Color	Time	Temperature

Concluding Statement:

1. Write a conclusion regarding the effects of surface color on temperature when exposed to sunlight. Support your views.

    _____

    _____

    _____

Name: _____ Date: _____

Student Inquiry Activity 2: Heating of Earth's Atmosphere/ Surface (cont.)

Part 2 – How Are Rates of Heating Impacted by the Earth's Substances?

Challenge: Think about how the temperature of various materials on the earth's surface would react to warming by sunlight. Do you think all materials would heat evenly? Why or why not? Design a controlled investigation to determine the effects of sunlight on the temperature of various substances found on the earth's surface. A sample guide is provided below.

What are the effects of the type of earth substance receiving sunlight on the temperature of the earth substance?

My hypothesis (do this part individually): _____

_____

_____

Materials needed/used: _____

_____

_____

Variables we controlled: _____

_____

_____

Procedures we followed: _____

_____

_____

_____

Data collected: _____

_____

_____

Analysis (What does the data collected mean to me?): _____

_____

_____

_____

Conclusion (Recheck your hypothesis): _____

_____

_____

_____

Name: _____ Date: _____

Student Inquiry Activity **2**: Heating of Earth's Atmosphere/ Surface (cont.)

Summary/What to Look For:

Part 1:

1. To what extent did students recognize the variation of temperature according to the color of the surface?
2. To what extent were students able to extend this principle to everyday life contexts, particularly weather-related?
3. In what ways were students' prior understandings altered by the activity?

Part 2:

1. To what extent was the inquiry investigation valid, e.g., use of the scientific method?
2. To what extent were students able to associate the variance in the heating of substances to the impact on our weather?

Discussion Questions/Assessment:

Part 1:

1. In what ways were your predictions accurate? Inaccurate? What may have been the cause of the inaccuracies?

   _____

   _____

   _____

   _____

2. How might the results affect your decision of which color of clothing to wear on a hot, sunny day?

   _____

   _____

   _____

   _____

3. Based on your findings, identify real-world examples of how the temperature of a surface is impacted by the color of the surface.

   _____

   _____

   _____

   _____

Name: _____ Date: _____

Student Inquiry Activity 2 : Heating of Earth's Atmosphere/Surface (cont.)

4. What do you believe causes a difference in the temperature of surfaces with different colors?

_____

_____

_____

_____

_____

5. What implications do the findings have for our weather? _____

_____

_____

_____

_____

_____

Part 2:

1. In what ways were your hypotheses accurate? In what ways will your hypotheses need to be adjusted?

_____

_____

_____

_____

_____

2. How did your findings compare with other groups? Were their findings similar? If not, speculate why.

_____

_____

_____

_____

_____

Name: _____ Date: _____

Student Inquiry Activity 2: Heating of Earth's Atmosphere/ Surface (cont.)

3. Think about swimming pools in fall and spring. What applications from this activity do you see regarding the temperature of the water?

_____

_____

_____

_____

_____

_____

4. What characteristics of water may cause it to cool and heat at rates different from other substances? (e.g., compare and contrast the substances you tested.)

_____

_____

_____

_____

_____

_____

_____

5. How are the findings from both activities related to our weather? _____

_____

_____

_____

_____

_____

_____

_____

_____

Name: _____ Date: _____

Student Inquiry Activity 3 : Where Did It Go?

Topic: Weather—Evaporation

Introductory Statement:

What happens to water when it disappears? In this activity, you will observe water as it disappears and try to explain where it goes when it disappears.

NSES Content Standard D: Structure of the Earth System

The atmosphere is a mixture of nitrogen, oxygen, and trace gases that include water vapor. The atmosphere has different properties at different elevations.

Global patterns of atmospheric movement influence local weather. Oceans have a major influence on climate, because the water in the oceans holds a large amount of heat.

Science Skills and Concepts:

- Students will observe the effects of evaporation.
- Students will predict the causes of evaporation.
- Students will infer that water can move from one state to another within the context of weather.
- Students will describe the processes of water evaporating.

Materials/Safety Concerns:

plastic picnic plates	crayons	traffic cones
string/twine	rulers	colored pencils
sidewalk chalk (various colors)	flexible tape measure	thermometers
anemometer	compass	
science journals and/or student data recording sheets		

Content Background:

To better understand our weather, it is important that the students are aware of the various phase-changes of water. This activity is designed to focus on **evaporation**, the moving of water from a liquid to a gaseous state below its boiling point. Evaporation can be somewhat obscure for students as they are not usually able to observe it directly. However, students will likely have observed the effects of evaporation (e.g., puddles drying up, condensation disappearing from windows and mirrors, sweat disappearing without being wiped away, etc.). Students may mistakenly assume that the water simply goes away when it evaporates.

Most of the water in the atmosphere comes from evaporation. Although more slowly than land, water absorbs heat energy from the incoming radiant energy. Evaporation requires heat energy. As water evaporates, its molecules move more quickly than when it was a liquid. The energy absorbed is stored in vaporous molecules as **latent** (meaning hidden) **heat**. In weather terms, this is important later in the water cycle as the latent heat is released during condensation.

Name: _____ Date: _____

Student Inquiry Activity **3** : Where Did It Go? (cont.)

Please note: Evaporation is best studied in conjunction with **condensation** (a reverse process), especially as they occur within the context of weather. This lesson specifically focuses on evaporation; the following two lessons will address condensation as relative humidity and dew point are studied. The application of these concepts can then be applied to the study of the water cycle, the essence of all weather.

Management Tip: For teachers in departmentalized settings, perhaps this activity could be started by one class and checked periodically by students from subsequent classes throughout the day.

Procedures:
1. Arrange students into the groups of your choice. Begin with an opportunity for the students to define:
   • what they believe to be the process of evaporation.
   • what causes evaporation.
   • the effects of evaporation.
   • samples of life experiences with evaporation.

   This could be done in large- or small-group format or in journals; space is provided for student response. Identify any naive conceptions the students may have at this point.

2. Explain that when studying weather, we often must watch for evidence of science principles. We can't always see things in science with our naked eye, but we can observe the effects of many weather principles; evaporation is a good example.

3. This activity can be done indoors or outdoors. It is recommended to complete the activity in both places for later comparison. This activity consists of a small amount of set-up time and extended periods of data recording. It allows for other activities to be done as long as data collection opportunities are provided for every hour throughout the day.

Indoor Set-up:
Set a plastic picnic plate in an area where it will not be disturbed by everyday classroom traffic. Pour a small amount of water onto the plate so the bottom of the plate is at least 75 percent covered. Because of the adhesion of the water and plastic and possible imperfections of the plate, you will likely observe the water pooling in some non-uniform shape. Instruct students to use dark-colored crayons to carefully trace the outline of the small puddle of water. Have students record the time and corresponding color of crayon; this is important because later a new color of crayon will be used. Instruct students to re-trace and label the puddle every hour throughout the day using a different color of crayon each time. Instruct students to measure the temperature and relative humidity each hour throughout the day. Encourage them to record both qualitative and quantitative observations as data is collected.

Name: _____ Date: _____

Student Inquiry Activity 3 : Where Did It Go? (cont.)

Indoor Setup:

Option: To simulate wind, the indoor evaporation can be expedited by placing the plates in the direct line of a fan.

Outdoor Set-up

Ideally, this activity is best suited for a relatively flat, hard surface (e.g., playground, tennis court, parking lot, etc.). Watch for the creation of puddles of water left after a heavy rain; a hose can be used to create puddles in dry periods. The activity works best on high-pressure, clear, breezy days.

Outdoor Setup:

Repeat the directions above, but substitute sidewalk chalk as a marker each hour throughout the day. It is recommended to cordon off the puddle area if possible; perhaps use traffic cones and twine to create a barrier to prevent disturbance to the puddle.

For outdoor set-ups, record overall weather conditions each hour, including wind speed/direction, temperature, percentage/types of clouds, relative humidity, etc.

4. Following data collection, analyze the results by discussing the findings and observations made from the data collecting period. Encourage students to hypothesize what happened to the water. Ask students to refer to their preliminary thoughts (see Step 1). Point out that matter can neither be created nor destroyed. Guide the discussion to include the phase-change of water to a gas. Introduce the term **water vapor** and emphasize that it is not visible to the naked eye. Conclude that the water must now be somewhere in the atmosphere. Ask students to share their views of how evaporation fits into weather. Close the lesson with an offer for students to modify any previous views, if needed. Encourage the sharing of incorrect assumptions that have been altered.

Name: _____ Date: _____

Student Inquiry Activity 3 : Where Did It Go? (cont.)

Exploration/Data Collection:

Where Did It Go?

Group Members: _____

Please write a brief description of your thoughts regarding the following:

1. Describe what you believe to be the process of evaporation. _____

   _____

   _____

   _____

   _____

2. What do you believe causes evaporation? _____

   _____

   _____

   _____

3. What are the effects of evaporation? _____

   _____

   _____

   _____

   _____

4. What are some examples of evaporation in your daily life? _____

   _____

   _____

   _____

5. Draw a diagram of what you believe happens to water when it evaporates.

29

Name: _____ Date: _____

Student Inquiry Activity 3 : Where Did It Go? (cont.)

Data Collection:

Indoor Set-up:

1. Measure and record a diagram of the water puddle each hour. You can either use one diagram and add a different-colored crayon for each hour, or you can draw a new puddle each hour. Either way, be sure to label the puddle time and relative measurements, e.g., how many centimeters across.

2. Observations I have made. _____

_____

_____

_____

_____

Outdoor Set-up (if applicable):

1. Diagram:

2. Observations I have made. _____

_____

_____

_____

_____

30

Name: _____ Date: _____

Student Inquiry Activity 3 : Where Did It Go? (cont.)

Summary/What to Look For:
1. To what extent are prior conceptions altered as a result of the activities and related analyses, conclusions, and discussions?
2. To what extent is weather mentioned when real-life examples of evaporation are listed (compare pre- vs. post-)?
3. To what extent are students able to describe what happens to water molecules during the phase-change from liquid to gas?

Discussion Questions/Assessment:
Answer the following questions on your own paper.

1. Where do you think the water went? Why do you believe this happened?

2. In what ways did the results from the indoor set-up differ from the outdoor set-up? What factors may have contributed to the differences, if any?

3. Why do you believe you can no longer see the water?

4. What would happen to our weather if there was no longer any evaporation?

5. What are some other examples of evaporation in your everyday life?

6. What could you do to increase the rate of the evaporation of the water? Decrease the rate of the evaporation of the water?

7. Which container would allow evaporation to occur faster on a sunny day: 5 liters of water in a tall narrow tube or 5 liters of water poured onto the driveway? Explain.

Name: _____ Date: _____

Student Inquiry Activity 4 : Where Did It Come From?

Topic: Weather—Condensation

Introductory Statement:

Recall that in the last lesson, you determined where water went when it seemed to disappear. In these activities, you will see water "reappear" and explain what conditions are necessary for this to happen.

NSES Content Standard D: Structure of the Earth System

The atmosphere is a mixture of nitrogen, oxygen, and trace gases that include water vapor. The atmosphere has different properties at different elevations.

Clouds, formed by the condensation of water vapor, affect weather and climate.

Science Skills and Concepts:

- Students will measure dew points.
- Students will observe condensation.
- Students will describe the process of condensation and how it relates to our weather (atmospheric conditions).

Materials/Safety Concerns:

Tin cans (soup cans will work well, but be cautious of sharp edges)
Ice cubes   Water
Spoons (for stirring)   Thermometers (alcohol)
Crayons/markers   12″ x 18″ white construction paper
Clear 2-liter soda bottle   Large sheets of white freezer paper
Matches   Weather-related reference resources
     (see book list)

Content Background:

A key phase in the water cycle is **condensation**, the movement of water from a gaseous state to a liquid state. In the previous lesson that featured evaporation, a key question was, "Where did it (water) go?" Within the context of phase-changes of matter, condensation can be thought of as the opposite of evaporation. Therefore, a logical question regarding condensation might be, "Where did it come from?"

Recall that one form of water existing in our atmosphere as a gas (water vapor) is invisible. It is impossible for students to directly observe water vapor. However, students can directly observe the results of condensation, e.g., water droplets forming on the outside of a cool metal surface. Students can also directly observe the results of condensation within the context of weather, specifically the formation of clouds. Condensation is the basis by which clouds are formed, both in the sky and near the ground as fog. In order for clouds to form, three ingredients are necessary: water vapor, condensation nuclei, and cooling. As water vapor cools, it reaches saturation point and condenses around tiny particles of dust, smoke, and other particulates within the atmosphere. Condensed water appears as tiny water droplets. Large groups of tiny water drops appear as clouds. All clouds are formed by the same physical process (phase-

Name: _____ Date: _____

Student Inquiry Activity **4** : Where Did it Come From? (cont.)

change); however, the types of clouds will vary depending upon the atmospheric conditions. Depending upon the temperature, the tiny water droplets may freeze or remain in a liquid state. This is why most high-level clouds are tiny particles of ice, even though they appear to be white. Closer to earth, condensation can be observed in the form of dew on the grass or frost, if the temperature is below freezing.

Condensing water vapor from the exhaust of jet engines forms condensation trails, often called **contrails**. Students may infer the amounts of moisture at high altitudes by observing

how quickly contrails disappear. If a contrail is very short and evaporates quickly, atmospheric moisture levels at that particular altitude must be relatively dry. Conversely, if the contrail remains visible and spreads out across the sky, one can infer that atmospheric moisture levels at that particular altitude must be relatively high. The direction of winds aloft may also be inferred by noting the direction in which the contrails spread from the

original path of the plane. Students may also infer cloud heights by gauging the vertical position of contrails as they intersect clouds.

Teachers are encouraged to watch for the students' application of knowledge of evaporation and relative humidity as these investigations are conducted.

Procedures:

This lesson features four parts and may take several days to complete. In Part 1, students calculate dew points and observe condensation forming on the outside of a tin can. Part 2 consists of a cloud-forming activity. Part 3 is an ongoing data collection activity regarding cloud types and related weather features. In Part 3, student data collection sheets are left to the teacher's preferences. Part 4 is an investigation into condensation trails. Students observe contrails and compare/contrast them with clouds.

Part 1—Dew Point:

1. Briefly review information discovered as a result of the investigations with evaporation. Explain that we left water in a gaseous state called water vapor and that it is now invisible. Announce that we are going to see what happens to the water vapor when it is cooled.

2. Entertain discussion about temperature differences from the earth's surface upward, e.g., what happens to the temperature as altitude increases? Some students may have experienced high altitudes and/or flight and will be aware that the temperature drops with altitude. Others may mistakenly assume that temperatures increase with altitude because you are getting closer to the sun.

3. Place students into the groups of your choice. Distribute materials needed to calculate dew point (soup cans, ice, water, thermometers). Instruct students to fill the soup cans approximately half-full of water and record the temperature of the water as well as the temperature of the air. Students should gradually add ice to the water, stirring continuously; this represents cooling. **Warning:** Do not stir with thermometers. Record the drop in the temperature of the water every 30 seconds. Ask students to make additional observations as more ice is added and stirred in the soup can. Students may observe condensation

Name: _____ Date: _____

Student Inquiry Activity 4 : Where Did it Come From? (cont.)

forming on the outside of the can. The temperature at which condensation occurs is known as the **dew point**. If students did not record this as an observation, have them repeat the process and watch carefully for the formulation of condensation. Students may discover that rubbing their fingers along the side of the can better reveals the condensation forming.

4. Discuss student perceptions of what occurred: What happened to the outside of the can? Where did the water come from? How are dew point and humidity related?

Part 2—Cloud in a Bottle:

This activity can be used as a teacher demonstration, or students can work in small groups to create their own clouds.

1. Place one to two ounces of water in the soda bottle. Swish the water completely around in the bottle.
2. Pour most of the water out of the bottle leaving only enough to cover the bottom of the bottle.
3. With the cap of the soda bottle removed, light a match; after it burns for a second or two, hold the match near the opening of the bottle, and blow the match out. Catch some of the smoke of the match in the bottle. Quickly put the cap tightly on the bottle.
4. Squeeze the side of the bottle hard.
5. Quickly release the pressure on the bottle.
6. Look for a thin cloud to form in the bottle. Holding the bottle against a darker background may make the cloud easier to observe.
7. Students may be able to continue to squeeze and release the bottle a number of times in order to observe the cloud being formed.

Part 3—Cloud Observation and Identification:

1. Encourage students to individually record their beliefs about what causes clouds. Provide prompts as needed: Where do clouds come from? How are clouds formed?
2. Cloud types vary depending on atmospheric conditions. The goal of this section is to have students make observations of clouds in conjunction with other pertinent weather data. Daily, students should systematically collect data on cloud types (using cloud identification charts). In addition, encourage students to record temperature, relative humidity, dew point, barometric pressure, and wind direction and speed. Chart the data so that cloud types can be analyzed as they pertain to the related weather conditions. Challenge students to ultimately make generalizations about how cloud types can tell us about the type of weather that occurs concurrently (e.g., cumulus clouds are associated with fair weather and high pressure; stratus clouds are associated with rainy weather and low pressure).

Part 4—Condensation Trails:

(**Note:** The success of this activity is dependent upon the availability of observable condensation trails left by jets. Local geography may dictate whether this activity is suitable.)

1. Encourage students to observe the sky and record observations in their science journals. Lead a large-group discussion about what they observed. Accept student responses, and create a list of their responses on large sheets of freezer paper. Classify the list into two

Name: _____ Date: _____

Student Inquiry Activity 4 : Where Did it Come From? (cont.)

main categories: natural and manmade. Watch for and focus on any mention of airplanes and/or condensation trails. Note the terminology used by students, e.g., what do they call the contrails? Avoid introducing the phrase "contrails"; rather, use the terminology as proposed by the students. Return outside to observe the sky, this time focusing only on the contrails. Ask students to write what they believe to be the cause of condensation trails. Ask students to compare and contrast clouds and contrails. Use prompts such as:

- What are the differences and similarities between clouds and contrails?
- Which are higher, clouds or contrails? How do you know?
- What causes contrails?
- In what ways do contrails vary? Why do you think this is the case?
- Would a small plane produce contrails? Why or why not?

2. When appropriate, introduce the phrase "condensation trail." Using the information learned about condensation in Parts 1–3 above, encourage students to examine their written explanations for accuracy. Instruct them to create a drawing that demonstrates the role of condensation in contrails. Provide reference materials that contain information regarding contrails. Perhaps this is a good question for "Ask Jeeves for Kids" (www.ajkids.com).

Exploration/Data Collection:
Part 1—Where Do Clouds Come From?:
1. Record the temperature of the air. _____

2. Record the original temperature of the water before ice is added. _____

3. Record the temperature of the water at 30-second intervals as ice is added and stirred into the water.

_____

_____

4. Record your observations.

_____

_____

_____

Part 2—Cloud in a Bottle:
1. Follow directions as given by your teacher. Describe what you observe. _____

_____

_____

_____

_____

Name: _____ Date: _____

Student Inquiry Activity ▮4▮ : Where Did it Come From? (cont.)

2. Record what you believe caused the cloud to form in the bottle. _____

    _____

    _____

    _____

    _____

3. Check the cloud 20 minutes later. Record and explain what you observe. Include where you believe the cloud went.

    _____

    _____

    _____

    _____

Part 3—Cloud Observation and Identification:

1. Write about what you believe to be the cause of clouds (e.g., how are they formed?).

    _____

    _____

    _____

    _____

    _____

2. Each day, observe the characteristics of the clouds in the sky. Also, record the temperature, relative humidity, barometric pressure, and wind speed and direction. Using a cloud chart, identify the type(s) of clouds you observed. Hint: Arrange your data in the form of a table. This will enable you to look for patterns in the data you have collected. After a period of two to three weeks, are you able to notice any relationships between the data? Explain.

    _____

    _____

    _____

    _____

    _____

Name: _____ Date: _____

Student Inquiry Activity **4**: Where Did it Come From? (cont.)

Part 4—Trails in the Sky:

1. Go outdoors and choose a comfortable spot as assigned by your teacher. Spend 5–10 minutes looking up into the sky. Record your observations below. If necessary, draw a picture and/or a diagram on your own paper that can help clarify your observations. Remember to use your five senses.

_____

_____

_____

_____

2. Following your class discussion, return to your spot outdoors and focus on the large, white streaks in the sky. Think about the following questions:

   • What are the differences and similarities between clouds and the large, white streaks?
   • Which are higher, clouds or the large, white streaks? How do you know?
   • What causes the large, white streaks?
   • In what ways do the large, white streaks vary? Why do you think this is the case?
   • Would a small plane produce the large, white streaks? Why or why not?

3. On your own paper, create a drawing of what you observe. This time include labels and/or captions that can explain the large, white streaks relative to the questions you just answered. You may need to use reference materials to build a complete drawing. Be prepared to share your drawing with others.

Extension:

1. If clouds are made of tiny water droplets, why are clouds white? Why are they sometimes dark and ominous?

2. Why don't clouds fall from the sky?

Summary/What to Look For:

1. To what extent are students able to infer that the atmosphere contains moisture, both in liquid and gaseous states?
2. To what extent are students able to identify other life situations in which condensation occurs?
3. To what extent are students able to articulate the concept of water converting from gas to liquid?
4. To what extent are students able to describe the relationships between humidity and dew point?
5. To what extent are students able to describe the formation and dissipation of clouds by viewing a model?
6. To what extent are students able to identify condensation as the cause for contrails?

Name: _____ Date: _____

Student Inquiry Activity 4 : Where Did it Come From? (cont.)

Discussion Questions/Assessment: (Use your own paper if you need more room.)

1. Write about other situations where you have observed condensation forming.

   _____

   _____

2. In what way are humidity and dew point related? _____

   _____

   _____

3. What weather-related factors might cause the dew point to rise and fall?

   _____

   _____

4. Write weather statements that link cloud types to related weather conditions, e.g., what type of weather is associated with the various types of clouds you have observed?

   _____

   _____

   _____

5. Complete the dew point activity in the same locations where relative humidity is collected (see later lesson). What relationship do you see between humidity and dew point temperature?

   _____

   _____

   _____

6. T or F Contrails are clouds. Explain your reasoning; use diagrams if needed.

   _____

   _____

7. Present students with two demonstrations:
   • A glass of cool liquid so there is condensed water clearly visible on the outside
   • A chilled glass so there is frozen, condensed water on the outside (may need to replace frequently)

   Ask students to use narrative and/or drawings to explain what happened in context.

Name: _____ Date: _____

Student Inquiry Activity 5 : Falling From the Sky

Topic: Weather—Precipitation

Introductory Statement:

In this activity, you will consider water as it falls from the sky in both solid and liquid forms.

NSES Content Standard D: Structure of the Earth System

Water, which covers the majority of the earth's surface, circulates through the crust, oceans, and atmosphere in what is known as the "water cycle." Water evaporates from the earth's surface, rises and cools as it moves to higher elevations, condenses as rain or snow, and falls to the surface where it collects in lakes, oceans, soil, and in rocks underground.

Science Skills and Concepts:

- Students will state various forms of precipitation.
- Students will describe precipitation as it occurs in the water cycle.
- Students will infer types of precipitation inherent within weather systems.
- Students will classify snowflakes according to crystal type.

Materials/Safety Concerns:

drawing paper   colored pencils
small, 3″ x 3″ pieces of waxed paper   hand lenses, one per student
medicine droppers, one per student
student data sheets from "Where Did It Go?" and "Where Did It Come From?"
number of snowflake-catchers desired— 5″ x 5″ pieces of black felt and 5″ x 5″ pieces of thin, stiff cardboard
hot glue gun **(Caution: For safety, teachers should assist students with gluing.)**

Content Background:

Another key phase of the water cycle is precipitation. Precipitation is arguably the most prominent feature of the water cycle in our weather. It is directly observable by students and often affects their daily lives. The most common forms of precipitation include rain and snow. Perhaps less common forms include sleet, freezing rain, and hail. It is important for students to understand that **precipitation** occurs when water in liquid and solid form can no longer stay aloft. In short, precipitation is a direct extension of the force of gravity. Challenge students to consider temperature and upper atmospheric conditions as key indicators of the types of precipitation. The focus of these activities is limited to rain and snow; however, extensions could include other forms of precipitation as well.

In most regions of the world, rain begins as snowflakes and small ice particles high in clouds. As the ice and flakes fall, most melt and combine into raindrops. The tiny drops originate as round in shape, but flatten slightly on the bottom as they fall. If the force of gravity is great enough and the drop becomes large enough, a raindrop may actually split into two drops as it falls. Of course, if temperatures remain low enough throughout the fall, snowflakes will not melt

Name: _____ Date: _____

Student Inquiry Activity 5 : Falling From the Sky (cont.)

and will collect on the earth's surface. Types of snow crystals are dependent upon the temperatures at which they are formed. For example, while all snowflakes are six-sided, snowflakes formed at -15°C (5°F) will likely form six-sided crystals. Other types of crystals include six-sided, needle-like crystals and six-sided, tube-shaped crystals.

Procedures:
Part 1—Water Cycle Drawings:
1. Briefly review the findings from investigations of evaporation (Where Did It Go?) and condensation (Where Did It Come From?). Encourage students to illustrate their current understanding of these two concepts by drawing a diagram/picture of the processes. Have students label all parts of the drawing. As students work, watch for any naive conceptions, e.g., following evaporation, be sure water vapor is accounted for but invisible.
2. Lead a large-group discussion of student drawings. Encourage students to share what they drew and why. Listen for an opportunity to pose the question, "If water from the earth's surface evaporates and becomes part of the atmosphere, in what ways does it ever get returned?" Listen for mention of precipitation and arrive at a consensus for a class definition.
3. Encourage students to complete the water cycle drawings and label them as such. Allow students to edit their drawings as a result of the discussion, if needed.

Part 2—Raindrops:
1. Ask students to draw a series of raindrops, from clouds to the earth, on a sheet of white paper; allow the students to color the drops if they desire. Each student should draw his/her own and not compare with others. Many will likely draw a teardrop-shaped raindrop and color it blue. Check to see if the drops are consistent in shape from the top of the page to the bottom.
2. Point out that raindrops of 0.08 inches in diameter begin as spheres. Display a circle with a diameter of 0.08 inches to give students an idea of the size. You may wish to enlarge such a drop by drawing it on the chalkboard; be sure to mention that you are magnifying the spherical drop. Have students compare the size (diameter) and shape of their raindrops to the small circle. Discuss what may happen to raindrops as they fall through the air. One change may include an increase in size, if they combine as they fall. Another change may include shape as the bottom tends to flatten out because of increased air pressure under the drop (see drawing). Finally, large raindrops (0.25 inches in diameter) may split apart

Raindrops forming

and form two new smaller drops. Illustrate this by having students place drops of water on pieces of waxed paper and view it from the side (eye level).
3. On the back of the original drawing, encourage students to create a revised version of the series of raindrops, from clouds to the earth. Ask them to incorporate the changes a raindrop may go through as it falls from a cloud.

Student Inquiry Activity 5 : Falling From the Sky (cont.)

Part 3—Snowflakes (for winter applications):

1. Challenge students to create a drawing similar to Part 2, only substitute snowflakes. Instruct them to illustrate weather-related conditions that would dictate snow rather than raindrops, e.g., see if they adjust for the lower temperatures.

2. Lead a class discussion regarding indicators of whether it will rain or snow. Accept responses related to sleet and freezing rain, although try to direct the discussion to rain and snow, the two most common forms of precipitation.

3. Construct snowflake-catchers by hot-gluing pieces of black felt to stiff pieces of cardboard. Prior to observing snowflakes, place the snowflake catchers in the freezer, so when the snowflakes are "caught," they will not melt immediately. Go outdoors to catch and observe snowflakes. Use hand lenses to compare and contrast the snowflakes, e.g., size and shape. Use reference materials* to identify the types of crystal formations that were observed. While outdoors, record weather conditions that can be associated with the types of snowflakes. For further comparison, repeat the activity during times of heavy, wet snow and during times of dry, powdery snow.

4. Refer back to the original drawings (see Step 1). Encourage students to create a revised version of the snowflakes, from clouds to the earth.

*Note: a complete classification of snowflakes can be found at:

Carr, P. (January 1994). "From Snowflakes to Snowstorm." *Learning* (Learning Poster). Pitman Learning Inc., 19 Davis Drive, Belmont, CA 94002

Williams, J. (1997). *The Weather Book.* New York: Vintage Books. pp. 100–101.

Exploration/Data Collection:
Precipitation (Part 1):

1. On your own paper, create a drawing/diagram that illustrates *evaporation* and *condensation* of the earth's water. Be sure to label all important parts of your drawing. Feel free to add color as needed. Please use only one side of the sheet for your drawing; you may turn the sheet on its side if you prefer.

Precipitation (Part 2):

1. On your own paper, create a drawing/diagram that illustrates raindrops as they fall from clouds to the earth. Be sure to label all important parts of your drawing. Feel free to add color as needed. Please use only one side of the sheet for your drawing; you may turn the sheet on its side if you prefer.

Name: _____ Date: _____

Student Inquiry Activity 5 : Falling From the Sky (cont.)

Precipitation (Part 3):
1. On your own paper, create a drawing/diagram that illustrates snowflakes as they fall from clouds to the earth. Be sure to label all important parts of your drawing. Feel free to add color as needed. Please use only one side of the sheet for your drawing; you may turn the sheet on its side if you prefer.

Summary/What to Look For:
1. To what extent are students able to accurately illustrate precipitation within the context of the water cycle?
2. To what extent are students able to identify weather conditions that would dictate whether it would rain or snow?
3. To what extent are students able to accurately illustrate raindrops and snowflakes?

Discussion Questions/Assessment:
1. Compare your first drawing of raindrops with the second drawing. Write about the changes you made to the second drawing, and explain why you made these changes.

_____

_____

_____

_____

_____

2. One morning, Tina notices that it is snowing lightly even though the temperature outside was 2°C (35°F). Most of the snow melted as soon as it hit the ground. Tina is puzzled by what she is seeing. You can help Tina by explaining how it could be snowing even though the temperature is above the freezing point. How would you explain the situation?

_____

_____

_____

_____

_____

Name: _____ Date: _____

Student Inquiry Activity 6 : Relatively Speaking

Topic: Weather—Relative Humidity

Introductory Statement:

In this activity, you will determine how to measure the amount of moisture in the air, relative to how much it could hold if it were completely saturated.

NSES Content Standard D: Structure of the Earth System

The atmosphere is a mixture of nitrogen, oxygen, and trace gases that include water vapor. The atmosphere has different properties at different elevations.

Science Skills and Concepts:

- Students will measure and record relative humidity.
- Students will infer factors that influence the relative humidity of a body of air.
- Students will infer the relationship between relative humidity and precipitation within the context of the water cycle and weather.

Materials/Safety Concerns:

Sling psychrometers   Relative humidity charts
Thermometers   Athletic shoe shoestring
Manila folders

Content Background:

The previous lessons focused on water in a phase-change from liquid to gas (evaporation) and gas to liquid (condensation). This lesson is designed to examine how moisture in the atmosphere is measured.

Students may be aware of moisture in the atmosphere in terms of humidity. The very existence of moisture in the atmosphere suggests that we should be able to measure the amounts of humidity at given temperatures. **Relative humidity** (reported as a percentage) is defined as the amount of moisture in the air relative to what it could hold if it were entirely saturated at a given temperature. The relative humidity is important to know when watching for precipitation.

Procedures:

1. Lead a large-group review of concepts/conclusions gained from the previous lessons regarding evaporation, condensation, and the water cycle. Specifically, discuss the phase-changes of water represented in each of the lessons and activities. Ask each student to pretend that he/she is a meteorologist and has been called upon to report the amounts of moisture in a body of air. Have him/her record how each would proceed and what each would report. Examine these statements for any naive conceptions the students may have, such as "water vapor occurs as fog."

2. Review basic percentages and explain that one way to measure relative humidity is by using a device called a **psychrometer**; demonstrate the parts and how it works (see basic description below). If you do not have access to sling psychrometers, a similar setup is easily designed. Simply lay two thermometers side by side. Compare the temperatures to insure that they are properly calibrated. Measure and record the temperature of the air at

Student Inquiry Activity 6 : Relatively Speaking (cont.)

this point in time. Cut a small (2 cm) section of hollow shoestring (a flat shoestring will not work) and slip it over the end of one of the thermometers. Soak the small piece of shoestring with water. Carefully, yet vigorously, fan the ends of the two thermometers with a manila folder for a period of several minutes. Have students measure and record the temperatures on both thermometers. Using this data, consult a relative humidity chart (see page 47).

3. Explain that relative humidity is the amount of moisture in a body of air relative to what it could hold if it were entirely saturated at a given temperature. This is an excellent opportunity to discuss that air at different temperatures is capable of holding varying amounts of moisture. For example, as air cools, it is not able to hold as much moisture. Illustrate this principle by asking about students' experiences with dew/frost. They will affirm that it largely occurs at night. Students may also recall feeling damp when camping out at night. Relative humidity tends to rise at night and decrease during the day, despite the amount of moisture remaining the same (remember, what varies is the temperature).

4. Next, challenge students to practice measuring the relative humidity in various locations and temperatures throughout the building and school grounds. Strive for locations that would likely vary in temperature and moisture. Some examples follow:

- classroom
- locker room (preferably after showers have been running)
- an air-conditioned room
- boiler room
- various floors/levels if applicable
- gymnasium
- stairwell
- outside

In addition, encourage students to record anecdotal observations about the setting in which the relative humidity was measured.

Note: Teachers in departmentalized settings could perhaps track data throughout the day. This will provide some excellent data for follow-up discussions the next day: e.g., students in second period can compare their findings with those of the students in seventh period.

5. Have students pool their data for large-group analysis and conclusions. Observe for variance among the data. Strive to identify possible cause/effect relationships based on observations made and reported.

6. Assign students to search for an application of relative humidity in weather reports (broadcasts, newspaper, and Internet sites) especially as it relates to precipitation.

Name: _____ Date: _____

Student Inquiry Activity 6 : Relatively Speaking (cont.)

Exploration/Data Collection:

Relatively Speaking

Group Name: _____

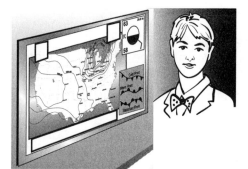

Help!!! … As a highly-trained, expert meteorologist, you have been summoned to report the relative humidity just outside your weather station. In addition, a request has been made for a brief description of how others could do the same. Good luck!

_____

_____

_____

_____

_____

****

The Quest for Relative Humidity

1. Our Relative Humidity Location _____

2. Dry Bulb Temperature   _____

3. Wet Bulb Temperature   _____

4. Depression Temperature   _____
   (subtract lowest from highest)

5. Relative Humidity (Use the chart on page 47.)   _____

6. Observations about our setting include:

_____

_____

_____

_____

_____

_____

Name: _____ Date: _____

Student Inquiry Activity 6 : Relatively Speaking (cont.)

Extension Inquiry:

1. Investigate the relationship between the time of year (season) and moisture levels in your house. Why does the air seem drier during some times of the year? What problems does this cause humans? In what ways do humans control these problems?

Summary/What to Look For:

1. To what extent are students able to accurately measure relative humidity?
2. To what extent are students able to identify relationships between temperature and relative humidity?
3. To what extent are students able to determine the relationships between relative humidity and various forms of precipitation?
4. To what extent are students able to identify the interface between evaporation and condensation within the context of relative humidity?
5. Did students report relative humidity in a percentage?

Discussion Questions/Assessment:

1. In what ways is dew different from rain? In what ways are they the same?

   _____

   _____

   _____

   _____

   _____

2. Refer to the lesson where you watched puddles evaporate over a period of time. Pretend that on one day, the relative humidity is very high. On this particular day, how would the rate of evaporation be affected by the high relative humidity?

   _____

   _____

   _____

   _____

   _____

   _____

Name: _____   Date: _____

Student Inquiry Activity 6 : Relatively Speaking (cont.)

Relative Humidity Chart

Dry-Bulb Temp. (°C)	Relative Humidity (%)																			
	Difference Between Wet- and Dry-Bulb Temperature (°C)																			
	1°	2°	3°	4°	5°	6°	7°	8°	9°	10°	11°	12°	13°	14°	15°	16°	17°	18°	19°	20°
-10	67	35																		
-9	69	39	9																	
-8	71	43	15																	
-7	73	48	20																	
-6	74	49	25																	
-5	76	52	29	7																
-4	77	55	33	12																
-3	78	57	37	17																
-2	79	60	40	22																
-1	81	62	43	26	8															
0	81	64	46	29	13															
1	83	66	49	33	17															
2	84	68	52	37	22	7														
3	84	70	55	40	26	12														
4	85	71	57	43	29	16														
5	86	72	58	45	33	20	7													
6	86	73	60	48	35	24	11													
7	87	74	62	50	38	26	15													
8	87	75	63	51	40	29	19	8												
9	88	76	64	53	42	32	22	12												
10	88	77	66	55	44	34	24	15	6											
11	89	78	67	56	46	36	27	18	9											
12	89	78	68	58	48	39	29	21	12											
13	89	79	69	59	50	41	32	23	15	7										
14	90	79	70	60	51	42	34	26	18	10										
15	90	80	71	61	53	44	36	27	20	13	6									
16	90	81	71	63	54	46	38	30	23	15	8									
17	90	81	72	64	55	47	40	32	25	18	11									
18	91	82	73	65	57	49	41	34	27	20	14	7								
19	91	82	74	65	58	50	43	36	29	22	16	10								
20	91	83	74	66	59	51	44	37	31	24	18	12	6							
21	91	83	75	67	60	53	46	39	32	26	20	14	9							
22	92	83	76	68	61	54	47	40	34	28	22	17	11	6						
23	92	84	76	69	62	55	48	42	36	30	24	19	13	8						
24	92	84	77	69	62	56	49	43	37	31	26	20	15	10	5					
25	92	84	77	70	63	57	50	44	39	33	28	22	17	12	8					
26	92	85	78	71	64	58	51	46	40	34	29	24	19	14	10	5				
27	92	85	78	71	65	58	52	47	41	36	31	26	21	16	12	7				
28	93	85	78	72	65	59	53	48	42	37	32	27	22	18	13	9	5			
29	93	86	79	72	66	60	54	49	43	38	33	28	24	19	15	11	7			
30	93	86	79	73	67	61	55	50	44	39	35	30	25	21	17	13	9	5		
31	93	86	80	73	67	61	56	51	45	40	36	31	27	22	18	14	11	7		
32	93	86	80	74	68	62	57	51	46	41	37	32	28	24	20	16	12	9	5	
33	93	87	80	74	68	63	57	52	47	42	38	33	29	25	21	17	14	10	7	
34	93	87	81	75	69	63	58	53	48	43	39	35	30	28	23	19	15	12	8	5
35	94	87	81	75	69	64	59	54	49	44	40	36	32	28	24	20	17	13	10	7

Name: _____   Date: _____

Student Inquiry Activity 7 : Water Cycle in a Bag

Topic: Weather—Earth's Hydrologic Cycle or Water Cycle

Introductory Statement:

The earth's water cycle is responsible for all the precipitation on the earth. The water on the earth and in the atmosphere continuously moves throughout the earth and its atmosphere.

NSES Content Standards D: Earth in the Solar System
The sun is the major source of energy for phenomena on the earth's surface, such as the growth of plants, winds, ocean currents, and the water cycle.

Science Skills and Concepts:
• Students will observe changes in a closed system.
• Students will predict future events.
• Students will understand the process of evaporation and condensation of water and the role they play in the water cycle of the earth.

Materials:
Clear, resealable-style sandwich bag   Small medicine cup or similar small cup (1–3 oz.)
Food coloring   Water

Content Background:

The **water cycle**, or **hydrologic cycle**, explains how water exists and moves on the earth. To understand the water cycle, you must first understand that the amount of water on the earth is constant. The amount of water on the earth has remained the same since its formation. The state of matter—solid, liquid, or gas (vapor)—in which the water exists can and does change. The atmosphere can hold a varying amount of water, either as water vapor or as liquid or solid water in clouds or some form of precipitation. Much of the earth's water is contained by the oceans, lakes, rivers, ponds, and so on. This is the water that is most commonly visible to you. Water can also be contained in the ground in the form of **groundwater**. This groundwater may be hidden in underground aquifers or in-ground. Water on the earth can also be contained in plants and animals. About three-fourths of the human body is water contained in cells, tissues, and organs. Water in the solid state can also exist as glaciers and icebergs.

Most of the water that comes to the ground from the atmosphere arrives in some form of precipitation, such as rain, snow, dew, etc. The water that lands on the earth's surface may be

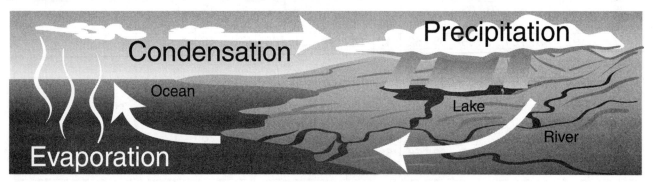

Name: _____ Date: _____

Student Inquiry Activity 7 : Water Cycle in a Bag (cont.)

either absorbed into the ground and become part of the groundwater system or might run into a lake, stream, pond, or some other body of water. The water in the atmosphere usually gets into the atmosphere by way of **evaporation**. This is the process by which the molecules of water in a liquid state move or vibrate with enough energy to be released from other water molecules and travel into the atmosphere. The temperature of the air determines the amount of water vapor the air can hold. Warmer air has a higher ability to hold water vapor than cooler air.

Procedure:
1. Fill the small cup about one-half full of water. Add a drop or two of red food coloring to the water.
2. Place the cup upright in one corner of the resealable bag as you hold the opposite corner of the bag up.
3. Seal the bag.
4. Tape the bag upright in a location that receives daily sunlight.
5. Observe the bag daily and record any changes you observe.

Exploration/Data Collection—The Water Cycle:
1. Record how the bag and water appear on Day 1 and each consecutive day.
2. Predict each day the changes you might observe.

Day 1. Observations.

_____

_____

_____

Prediction as to how it will appear tomorrow.

_____

_____

_____

Day 2. Observations.

_____

_____

_____

Prediction as to how it will appear tomorrow.

_____

_____

_____

Name: _____ Date: _____

Student Inquiry Activity 7 : Water Cycle in a Bag (cont.)

Day 3. Observations.

_____

_____

_____

Prediction as to how it will appear tomorrow.

_____

_____

_____

Day 4. Observations.

_____

_____

_____

Prediction as to how it will appear tomorrow.

_____

_____

_____

Day 5. Observations.

_____

_____

_____

Prediction as to how it will appear tomorrow.

_____

_____

_____

3. Explain the causes of any changes that you observed.

_____

_____

_____

_____

_____

Name: _____ Date: _____

Student Inquiry Activity 7 : Water Cycle in a Bag (cont.)

Summary/What to Look For:

Water in the cup will evaporate and become water vapor. As the temperature within the bag changes due to the amount of sunlight it receives, the ability of the air in the resealable bag to hold water vapor will also change. As the temperature in the bag decreases, the air's ability to hold water will decrease. Condensation of some of the water vapor will occur and flow to the lowest corner of the bag.

1. To what extent are students able to explain what happened within the bag?
2. To what extent are students able to relate what happened in the bag to the atmosphere?

Extensions:

1. Investigate whether the color of water has any effect on the evaporation/condensation process.

2. A thermometer could be placed inside the resealable bag, and one could be attached to the outside of the bag. Comparison of the two temperature readings could become part of the data collected each day.

3. Students could compare a saltwater cycle (solution of salt water) to regular water.

4. After completing the water cycle in the bag, students could design an enclosed terrarium and maintain the terrarium for an extended period of time.

Discussion Questions/Assessments:

1. Explain what happened to the color of the water.

_____

_____

_____

_____

_____

_____

2. Explain the similarity between a terrarium containing plants and the resealable bag.

_____

_____

_____

_____

_____

_____

Name: _____ Date: _____

Student Inquiry Activity 8 : What Pressure!

Topic: Weather—Barometric Pressure

Introductory Statement:

Recall from earlier discussions and activities that weather is all around us, all of the time. Air is a key part of our weather. In these activities, you will determine the importance of air in our weather, especially air masses that are very different.

NSES Content Standard D: Structure of the Earth System
The atmosphere is a mixture of nitrogen, oxygen, and trace gases. The atmosphere has different properties at different elevations.

Science Skills and Concepts:

- Students will describe the physical properties of air, e.g., takes up space, has mass, and fluid.
- Students will infer that since air has mass and volume, it must therefore exert pressure.
- Students will differentiate between air masses with high pressure and air masses with low pressure.
- Students will compare and contrast weather conditions associated with areas of high and low pressure.
- Students will collect and record barometric pressure and relate it to current weather conditions.
- Students will synthesize weather data, collected daily.

Materials/Safety Concerns:

Air pillows or plastic bubble sheets (often used as packaging material)
Tuna can or small soup cans (be cautious of sharp edges)

Aneroid barometer	Straws	Rubber bands
Glue	Large balloons	3″ x 5″ cards

Science journals or exploration/data collection sheets

Content Background:

Air has mass and volume. As a result, it exerts pressure. Air is also considered to be a **fluid** as it takes the shape of its container and can flow. The focus of this lesson is on air pressure in the form of barometric pressure, an essential concept in our weather. Meteorologists identify air masses of low pressure and high pressure as they track weather patterns and prepare forecasts. Barometric pressure is measured with a barometer. Today, aneroid barometers have largely replaced mercury barometers due to safety concerns; however, the data is still reported in units of inches. This dates back to the measurement of the inches that mercury would rise in an inverted tube at sea level. Aneroid barometers can be purchased at a reasonable price; however, students can easily build their own barometers with basic materials.

The weather conditions associated with air masses of varying pressures are very different. Areas of **high pressure** are usually associated with fair weather; whereas, areas of **low pressure** are commonly associated with stormy weather. Students should collect barometric pressure data several times per day in order to determine if the pressure is rising or falling. This information

Name: _____ Date: _____

Student Inquiry Activity 8 : What Pressure! (cont.)

will help in predicting the type of weather conditions that should follow. On weather maps, these air masses are labeled with a large "L" for low pressure and "H" for high pressure. Students' understanding of barometric pressure and the related weather conditions is crucial to the comprehension of fronts and their movement.

Procedures:

1. Distribute air pillows or sections of bubble sheets to students. Caution them not to pop the objects. Ask them to observe the objects and make/record statements they can defend regarding the properties of air. Pool the observations and discuss their validity. Check for understanding that air has mass and volume. Explain that air is yet another important part of weather that we cannot see. Perhaps relate the discussion to knowledge gained during the study of wind. Explain that this lesson will take into account large areas of air called air masses. These masses often cover several states at once.

2. Encourage students to individually record a definition of the word *pressure.* Check for naive conceptions. Have students react to the statement "True or False: Air has pressure," and explain this reasoning. Allow students to share their views. Look for opportunities to introduce students to an analogy of the earth's surface as the bottom of a large ocean of air. Instead of water in this ocean, consider it to be "an ocean of air." Just as water would have pressure, so too does the air. In fact, the pressure is the greatest at the bottom of the sea (sea level in the real world) but not so great that we would be crushed. As we gain altitude, the air becomes thinner, and the pressure decreases.

3. Demonstrate air pressure for students by use of a discrepant event. Place a 3" x 5" card on top of a glass of water. Hold your hand on the 3" x 5" card while you completely invert the glass. Slowly take your hand off of the card (you may wish to do this over a sink or tub, just in case!). Encourage students to explain what they observe. Check their explanations for the concept of air pressure holding the card up. Allow students to try the demonstration as well.

4. Meteorologists identify air masses as high and low pressure by aggregating barometric pressure data from weather reporting stations across the United States. After the barometric pressure data is plotted on a map, lines are drawn to connect areas of equal pressure. These lines are referred to as **isobars**, or lines of equal pressure. Barometric pressure decreases as one moves to the center of the low-pressure area; barometric pressure increases as one moves to the center of a high-pressure area.

Distribute barometric pressure maps. Students should complete the accompanying questions and infer an area of high pressure (West-Southwest) and an area of low pressure (Michigan). Students should infer patterns in barometric pressure by examining isobars.

5. Refer back to the large masses of air discussed earlier in the lesson; perhaps one of those masses of air is surrounding the school right now. Encourage students to build a device to measure the pressure of the air mass, a barometer. Apply the use of the barometers by measuring and recording the barometric pressure at least two times per day. As usual, use the barometric pressure (rising or falling) in conjunction with other data to search for weather patterns and specific conditions.

Student Inquiry Activity **8** : What Pressure! (cont.)

Exploration/Data Collection:

What Pressure!

1. Carefully examine the package of air. Record observations and inferences about the air in the package. Be sure to use more than just your sense of sight. Be prepared to share and discuss your views.

   _____

   _____

   _____

2. T or F   Air has pressure. Explain your reasoning. _____

   _____

   _____

   _____

3. Describe what you believe causes the card to stay on the upside-down cup. Explain your reasoning.

   _____

   _____

   _____

4. After trying this yourself, record any additional thoughts about what keeps the card on the upside-down cup.

   _____

   _____

   _____

5. List other instances you can think of in which air exerts pressure. _____

   _____

   _____

   _____

6. Mallory Meteorologist needs your help with interpreting the weather map that displays barometric pressure using lines called isobars. **Isobars** connect areas of equal barometric pressure, or the amount of pressure exerted on the surface of the earth. Mallory has begun charting the barometric pressure by writing the barometric pressure on the isobars; she has labeled the isobars in millibars.

Name: _____ Date: _____

Student Inquiry Activity **8** : What Pressure! (cont.)

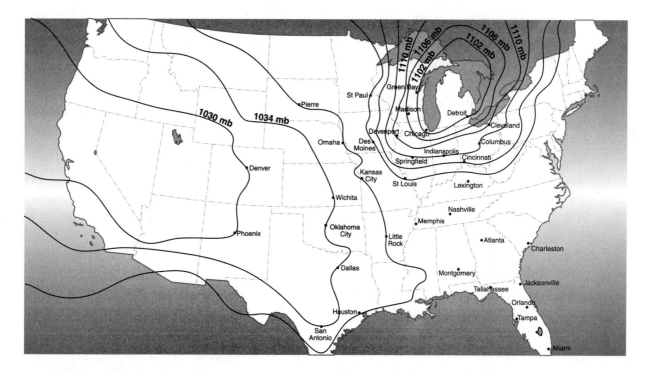

a. Help Mallory finish labeling the isobars that run through these cities:
   - Springfield, IL; Indianapolis, IN; and Columbus, OH
   - St. Paul, MN; Des Moines, IA; and St. Louis, MO
   - Wichita, KS; Oklahoma City, OK; and Dallas and San Antonio, TX
   - Pierre, SD; Omaha, NE; Kansas City, MO; Little Rock, AR; and Houston, TX

b. Describe patterns you notice in the barometric pressure readings in the upper Midwest and the West-Southwest.

   _____

   _____

   _____

   _____

c. Identify an area of low pressure and an area of high pressure; write "L" for low and "H" for high on the map.

d. Based upon the barometric pressure, what type of weather is likely occurring in Michigan? In the West-Southwest? Explain your reasoning.

   _____

   _____

   _____

Name: _____ Date: _____

Student Inquiry Activity 8 : What Pressure! (cont.)

e. Using an aneroid barometer provided by your teacher, convert the readings in millibars to inches and include this data on the isobars.

7. Build your own barometer by following these simple directions. (See diagram below.)

Step 1. Cut a large balloon in half.

Step 2. Stretch the balloon over the top of a tin can; stretch it so it is tight.

Step 3. Have a partner hold the balloon tight while you apply one or more rubber bands.

Step 4. Cut a straw 6 cm in length. Cut one end at an angle to create a pointed edge.

Step 5. Glue the non-cut end of the straw to the middle of the stretched balloon on the top of the can.

Step 6. Fold a 3″ x 5″ card in half. Stand it on edge next to the straw pointer, and mark the point at which the straw pointer touches the card; label this "line 5." Measure every half-centimeter above and below and mark 6, 7, 8, 9, 10 going up, and 4, 3, 2, 1 going down. Write the word *high* near the number 10 and the word *low* near the number 1. Along one side, write the word *rising* with an arrow going up; along the other side, write the word *falling* with an arrow going down. See the diagram for help.

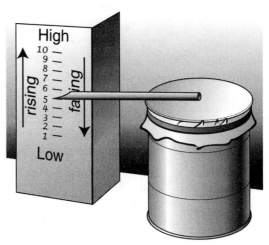

Step 7. Now you are ready to begin collecting data. Check the barometer in the morning and the afternoon; record the number by the straw pointer as well as "falling" or "rising" as it goes up and down. Compare your rising and falling data with that of data collected from a barometer provided by your teacher. This is called an aneroid barometer and has replaced more dangerous mercury barometers.

8. Be sure to consider the barometric pressure, along with other forms of weather data collected daily. For example, what types of weather conditions are present during times when the barometric pressure is falling and low? Rising and high? Why do you think this is the case?

_____

_____

_____

_____

_____

Student Inquiry Activity 8 : What Pressure! (cont.)

Summary/What to Watch For:
1. To what extent are students able to describe the physical properties of air? (mass, volume, exerts pressure)
2. To what extent are students able to infer that air exerts pressure by pushing down on the earth's surface?
3. To what extent are students able to accurately measure barometric pressure using both aneroid and homemade barometers?
4. To what extent are students able to associate low pressure with stormy, unstable weather patterns?
5. To what extent are students able to associate high pressure with fair, stable weather patterns?
6. To what extent are students able to associate changing pressure with changing weather?
7. To what extent are students able to synthesize data of weather conditions?

Extension:
1. Compare and contrast your barometric pressure data (teacher's barometer) with other sources of information (e.g., your local radio station, television station, newspaper, weather radio, National Weather Service, etc.). Explain why you believe there may be differences in the data.

Real-World Applications:
1. Think about daily decisions you make that might be altered if you had access to barometric pressure data.

Discussion Questions/Assessment: (Use your own paper for your responses.)
1. If you are trying to convince a friend that there is such a thing as air pressure, what would you tell him or her?

2. Using what you have learned about air pressure, explain how your homemade barometer works. Use diagrams and labels if needed.

3. Review the weather data, collected daily. What patterns do you see when looking at low/falling barometric pressure and overall weather conditions? For example, what types of weather do we experience during low pressure? High pressure?

Name: _____ Date: _____

Student Inquiry Activity **9** : Windy!

Topic: Weather—Measuring Wind

Introductory Statement:
Wind is a very important part of our weather. In many ways it can be helpful, but at other times it can be extremely harmful. In this activity, you will investigate the characteristics of wind and how to measure it.

NSES Content Standard D: Structure of the Earth System
Global patterns of atmospheric movement influence local weather.

NSES Content Standard D: Earth in the Solar System
The sun is the major source for phenomena on the earth's surface, such as the growth of plants, winds, ocean currents, and the water cycle.

Science Skills and Concepts:
• Students will identify manifestations of wind.
• Students will infer the effects of wind speed and direction on weather systems.
• Students will collect and analyze data regarding wind speed and direction.

Materials/Safety Concerns:
Construction paper	Scissors	Fishing swivel
Thread	Straight pins	Large, styrofoam cups (16 oz.)
Relatively new lead pencils with an eraser		Jumbo drinking straws
Manila folders, tagboard, or stiff cardboard		

Content Background:
Wind is a prime example of a weather concept that the students can't see but the effects of which they can observe. Not only can't they see wind, the processes that combine to cause wind are invisible and abstract as well. The students should realize that hot air rises from warm, tropical regions. This warm air rises and is deflected laterally as it cools, only to dive back down, creating wind belts that can be linked to geographical latitudes, e.g., tropical winds and polar winds. Older students may also be exposed to the deflection of winds caused by the spinning of the earth (Coriolis Effect), pressure gradient forces, and friction. **Pressure gradient forces** are pressure differences and lateral distance between high-pressure and low-pressure air masses. Meteorologists calculate pressure gradient forces as they prepare forecasts. In general, winds tend to blow in a clockwise direction and sink in areas of high pressure, which are often associated with fair weather. Conversely, winds tend to blow in a counterclockwise direction and rise in areas of low pressure. This can be observed by watching satellite loops commonly shown on weather broadcasts. Students can be reminded of this rule if they think of a screw, e.g., clockwise rotations cause the screw to go down; counterclockwise rotations cause the screw to rise.

Meteorologists are primarily concerned with two facets of wind as they prepare and deliver forecasts—speed and direction. These are key indicators of weather to come. In this activity, students will design and build data collection devices for wind speed and direction.

58

Name: _____ Date: _____

Student Inquiry Activity **9** : Windy! (cont.)

Procedures:

1. Discuss the causes of wind by questioning students about what they know of the tendencies of warm air as opposed to cold air. Cite real-life experiences, such as opening a refrigerator door (cold air tumbles out onto your feet). Warm air pours up and out the top of a door opened to the outside during cold weather (condensation occurs as warm, more moist air escapes out the top of the door). If possible, allow students to experience this by demonstrating.

2. As a large group, establish a definition for wind and cite the cause. Direct the discussion to the idea that wind is simply air that moves, and this is caused by differences in temperature. Perhaps reinforce the idea by setting up a convection demonstration. Cut a coil (2 cm wide) from construction paper. At the top, attach a short piece of thread between the coil and one end of a fishing swivel. Attach a second piece of thread to the other end of the fishing swivel. Demonstrate the rising movement of warm air by holding the coil above an open flame; it should begin to rotate. **Caution: Do not get the coil too close to the flame.**

3. Ask students to draw a globe and label the North and South Poles and the equator. Begin to introduce the vocabulary terms **polar** and **tropical regions**. Appeal to their sense of what types of clothing people would wear in each of these regions. Ask them to apply that knowledge when determining what type of air (cold and warm) would be found in each area. Encourage students to draw arrows to suggest the movement of the air. Demonstrate how wind belts are formed, e.g., air is deflected laterally as it rises, eventually sinking back down at the poles. Have students complete their drawings to reflect wind belts in both the northern and southern hemispheres.

4. Ask students to record their thoughts (in science journals) to the following question; "How do you know there is wind?" Provide students an opportunity to share their views with others. Record the essence of the discussion on poster paper. Point out that wind is a weather-related phenomena that we cannot see directly but the effects of which we can easily observe, especially in extreme cases. As a class, take a brief walk around the school grounds to "experience" wind. Students should record evidence of wind. Carefully discuss their observations and attempt to categorize some levels/degrees of strength. These classifications will be used during daily weather data gathering and charting.

A commonly accepted list of visual wind speed indicators is listed below:

Observation	Description	Miles Per Hour
smoke goes straight up	calm	1-3
smoke moves, but wind vane does not	light breeze	4-7
leaves rustle; wind felt on face	gentle breeze	8-12
leaves and small twigs move constantly; wind extends light flag	moderate breeze	13-18

Name: _____ Date: _____

Student Inquiry Activity 9 : Windy! (cont.)

Observation	Description	Miles Per Hour
small trees sway; small waves crest on lakes	fresh breeze	19-24
large branches move constantly; wires on electric poles hum	strong breeze	25-31
large trees sway; walking against wind is inconvenient	moderate gale	32-38
twigs break off large trees; walking against wind is difficult	fresh gale	39-46
branches break off trees; loose bricks blow off chimneys; shingles blow off	strong gale	47-54
trees snap or are uprooted; considerable damage to buildings is possible	whole gale	55-63
widespread damage to buildings	storm	64-75

Wind speed and direction are key weather data that should be systematically collected on a daily basis. This information is needed to infer weather patterns and relationships throughout the lessons; e.g., see "Relatively Speaking."

5. A simple wind vane can be constructed with inexpensive materials. Students should use their wind vanes to determine wind direction. Caution them to avoid areas of the school grounds where winds tend to swirl. Have students collect daily wind speed and direction data from various predetermined areas of the school grounds. Data can then be aggregated and used for analysis of weather patterns.

6. As students collect daily wind speed and direction data, encourage them to chart the data within the context of other forms of data (e.g., temperature, relative humidity, dew points, barometric pressure, cloud types, amounts and types of precipitation, etc.). Examine data collected over a period of weeks. Look for patterns in the data that would provide insight regarding weather systems.

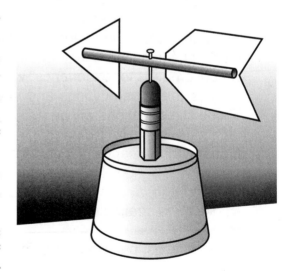

Student Inquiry Activity 9 : Windy! (cont.)

Exploration/Data Collection:
Wind, From What Direction and How Fast?

1. Record your individual definition of wind here. _____

   _____

   _____

2. Record your class definition of wind here. Compare it to your individual definition of wind.

   _____

   _____

   _____

3. How do you know there is wind? Explain your reasoning. _____

   _____

   _____

   _____

4. Record your observations of the evidence of wind. Remember to use more than just your sense of sight.

   _____

   _____

   _____

5. On your own paper, draw a large model of the earth (like a globe); locate and label the North Pole, the South Pole, and the equator. Mark areas on your model that would contain very warm air and very cold air. Include arrows to indicate the direction in which the air would move in both the Northern and Southern Hemispheres.

6. Directions to build a wind vane:
   a. Trace and cut out two pointers and fins (on tagboard) from the patterns on the next page. Glue the pointers and the fins together so they are symmetrical and surround roughly 4 cm of each end of the straw (see diagram on page 60).
   b. Invert a 16-oz. styrofoam cup and carefully bore a hole in the center with a thin, sharp object. The cup will serve as a holder/platform for the wind vane. Carefully insert the pointed end of a sharpened pencil; push the pencil down until it is level with the bottom of the inverted cup. The pencil should fit snugly in the hole that was created.
   c. Push a straight pin through the straw and mount it on the top of the pencil by pushing the pin into the eraser. Balance the straw with the pointer and fins so it is level and freely spins around in the wind. You may need to adjust the centering of the pin after testing it outdoors. Wind vanes will point to the direction from which the wind is blowing.

61

Name: _____ Date: _____

Student Inquiry Activity **9** : Windy! (cont.)

WIND VANE PATTERNS

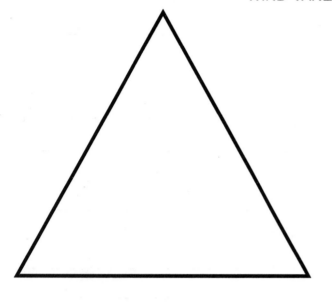
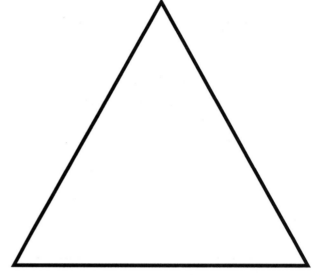

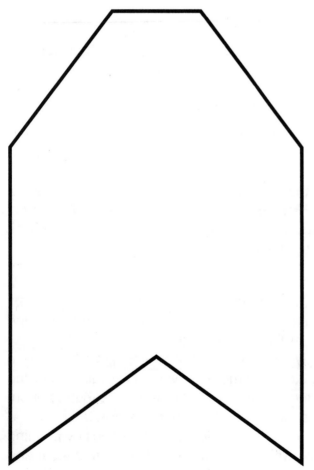
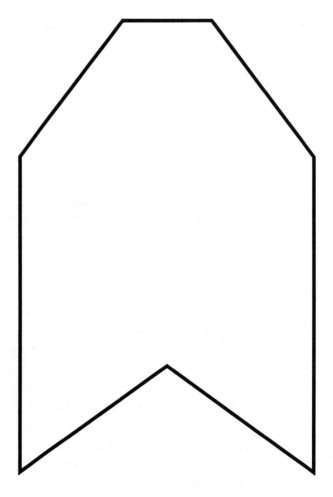

Name: _____ Date: _____

Student Inquiry Activity **9** : Windy! (cont.)

Extensions:

1. Compare and contrast your wind speed and direction data with other sources of information (e.g., your local radio station, television station, newspaper, weather radio, National Weather Service, etc.). Explain why you believe there may be differences in the data.
2. Research to find out the meaning of "wind chill." What other weather conditions are important with this term? How have wind chill calculations changed recently?
3. What would happen to the wind if the earth suddenly stopped spinning? Research to find information about something scientists call the *Coriolis Effect*.

Real World Applications:

1. Think about daily decisions you make that might be altered if you had access to wind speed and direction data.

Summary/What to Look For:

1. To what extent are students able to articulate the movement of air depending on its temperature (warm air rises; cold air sinks)?
2. To what extent have students accurately drawn a wind belt in each of the hemispheres?
3. To what extent are students able to accurately determine and record wind speed using visual observations?
4. To what extent are students able to determine wind direction using a simple wind vane?
5. To what extent are students able to associate wind conditions with other weather data?

Assessments:

1. On a sheet of poster board, build a collage of pictures taken from old magazines that would demonstrate that wind is present. You may add your own drawings to the collage, if necessary. Using visual observation indicators, label the approximate wind speed of the various pictures. Finally, include the direction in which the wind appears to be blowing; of course, this will depend on how the picture/drawing is positioned on your poster. Use north for the top of the poster, south for the bottom, east to the right, and west to the left.

2. Examine the weather data you have collected (as a whole); what patterns and/or relationships do you notice between wind speed and direction and the other data? Explain your reasoning.

_____

_____

_____

_____

_____

_____

Name: _____ Date: _____

Student Inquiry Activity 10 : Charting Weather Data

Topic: Interpreting Weather Maps

Introductory Statement:

In this activity, you will learn how to build and interpret "weather boxes," data that is contained on weather maps used by meteorologists.

NSES Content Standard D: Structure of the Earth System
Global patterns of atmospheric movement influence local weather.

Science Skills and Concepts:

• Students will plot weather data on a map.
• Students will infer weather conditions in cities, based on weather data.
• Students will use commonly accepted symbols to represent weather conditions on a map.

Materials:

A copy of a weather map and accompanying weather data chart

Content Background:

Students should be aware of the importance of communication in science. Weather-related concepts are no exception; meteorologists truly have a language of their own. **Weather boxes** are simply an organized collection of symbols used to represent the data. Weather boxes consist of a variety of weather data and are used to represent the weather conditions for a specific data collection location. This data is collected at National Weather Service stations via weather balloons, which are launched roughly every eight hours. Students might mistakenly assume that meteorologists use only computers to generate weather maps. Instead, National Weather Service personnel carefully create individual weather maps using colored pencils.

Weather boxes are positioned near the city on a weather map and contain the following information:

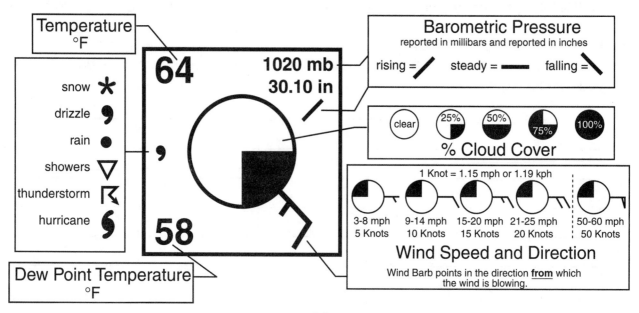

Student Inquiry Activity **10** : Charting Weather Data (cont.)

More sophisticated weather boxes may include cloud types, visibility, and the amount of change in barometric pressure in the past three hours. Most weather symbols have variations of the symbol to represent the intensity of the data.

Students can easily build basic weather boxes using existing weather conditions. Additionally, they can interpret weather conditions from existing weather boxes. These skills are important to their success with the capstone weather forecasting activity.

Procedures:

1. Ask students to offer suggestions regarding types of information that are needed to record weather data; urge them to recall past activities in order to formulate responses. Students are likely to offer such things as temperature, barometric pressure, wind speed, wind direction, cloud type, cloud cover, type of precipitation, etc.
2. Set a purpose for the lesson by suggesting that they learn a common language to communicate their findings. Stress the importance of communication and accurate data recording. Perhaps you could display copies of actual weather maps created by meteorologists.
3. Distribute the weather map and accompanying weather data chart. Review the main components of the weather box. Encourage students to complete the questions and provide assistance as needed.

Exploration/Data Collection:

Carefully examine and read the sample weather box provided on page 64.

Use the information provided in the weather boxes on the map on page 67 to answer the following questions.

1. What is the temperature in Des Moines, Iowa? _____

2. What is the wind speed in Atlanta, Georgia? _____

3. What type of a weather warning is likely being issued in Miami, Florida?

   _____

4. What is the wind direction in Oklahoma City, Oklahoma? _____

5. What is the barometric pressure in Columbus, Ohio? _____

6. Is the barometric pressure rising, falling, or remaining steady in Kansas City, Missouri? How do you know?

   _____

   _____

   _____

Name: _____ Date: _____

Student Inquiry Activity 10 : Charting Weather Data (cont.)

7. What is the percentage of cloud cover in Memphis, Tennessee? _____

8. What type of precipitation is occurring in St. Louis, Missouri? _____

9. From your understanding of fronts, draw a cold front on the map based on the information contained in the weather boxes.

10. From your understanding of barometric pressure, identify and label an area of stormy weather with very low pressure on the map.

11. Based on the understanding of weather conditions in Miami, Florida, what type of weather is likely to occur in Tampa in several hours? Explain your reasoning.

    _____

    _____

    _____

12. Explain why you think it is important for meteorologists to use weather boxes on weather maps.

    _____

    _____

    _____

13. Plot the data (from the chart below) on the map for the cities that are missing weather boxes. This time, you will need to create the weather boxes.

City	Cloud Cover	Temperature	Barometric Pressure	Type of Weather	Wind Speed/ Direction
San Antonio, TX	Clear	80	30.0 ↑	Sunny	5 mph SW
Denver, CO	100%	45	29.1 ↓	Snow	15 mph W
Milwaukee, WI	50%	35	30.1 steady		11 mph NW
Tampa, FL	75%	83	29.7 ↓	Thunderstorm	20 mph SE

Summary/Assessment:

1. To what extent did students accurately identify basic weather symbols?
2. To what extent did students accurately associate related weather conditions, e.g., low pressure and storms?
3. To what extent did students use prior understanding to successfully complete the map exercise?
4. To what extent did students articulate the need for a common language in weather data?

Name: _____ Date: _____

Student Inquiry Activity 10 : Charting Weather Data (cont.)

Weather Map

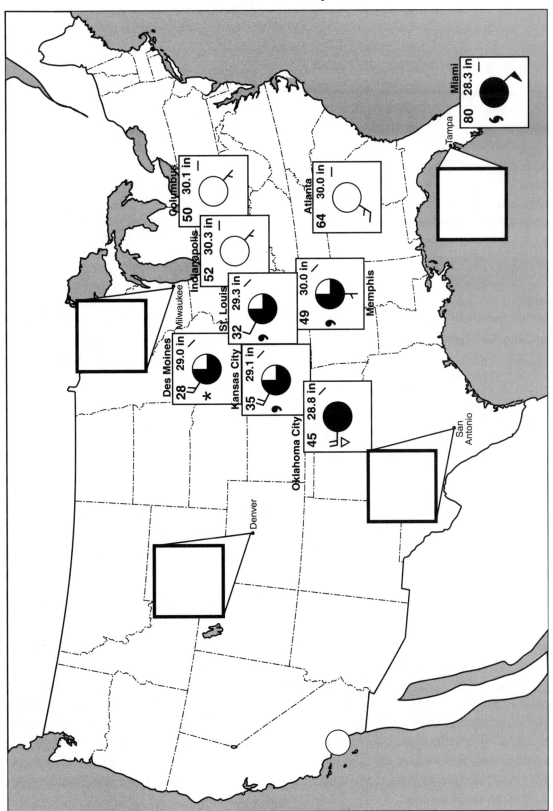

Name: _____ Date: _____

Student Inquiry Activity **11** : Where the Action Is

Topic: Weather—Fronts

Introductory Statement:

Identifying and tracking fronts is an important skill in accurately predicting the weather. In this activity, you will infer weather conditions based on the location and direction of fronts.

NSES Content Standard D: Structure of the Earth System
Global patterns of atmospheric movement influence local weather.

Science Skills and Concepts:

- Students will identify cold and warm fronts on a weather map.
- Students will compare and contrast cold and warm fronts.
- Students will describe the cause of cold, warm, and stationary fronts.
- Students will infer weather conditions with warm and cold fronts.

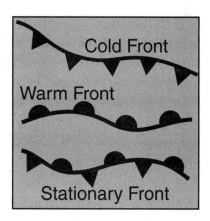

Materials:

Hand-drawn weather maps from a regional office of the
National Weather Service
Crayons or markers
A blank map of the United States

Background Content:

Students should become aware of two major types of fronts and the weather conditions associated with each. Weather fronts represent the movement of the air masses described in earlier lessons. **Fronts** are found along the leading edges of the air masses. The temperature and pressure of the encroaching air mass dictates the name of the front. For example, if a cold air mass overtakes a warm air mass, a **cold front** ensues. Typically, cold, dense air plows under warm, moist air, causing it to rise rapidly. Such a front is likely to yield a sudden, heavy rain shower as the warm, moist air is quickly cooled when it rises. Conversely, if a warm air mass overtakes a cold air mass, a **warm front** is created. The less dense, warm air tends to slide over the heavy, dense, cooler air. Stratus clouds often occur along with longer periods of steady rainfall. A third type of front (**stationary**) occurs when air masses tend to remain in one place for a period of time.

Fronts are where active weather occurs. Students will actually experience changes in the weather as fronts pass through. If the differences in the air masses are great, storms are spawned. Recall that high-pressure air masses tend to be associated with stable weather. Identification and understanding of encroaching air masses and fronts will help students predict weather. They can test their predictions by verifying the weather a day or two later. Most weather systems move from the west-southwest to east-northeast. Consequently, students should be aware of the direction and speed of moving air masses. Ideally, students should be able to accurately predict weather in other cities beyond their location, after the same weather has passed through their region.

Name: _____ Date: _____

Student Inquiry Activity **11** : Where the Action Is (cont.)

Procedures:

1. Ask students to record ideas of how to determine where warm and cold air masses are located throughout the United States. Watch for naive conceptions, e.g., warm air can only be found in the south because it is closer to the equator. Encourage students to share and discuss their views. One way meteorologists identify air masses is to chart relative temperatures. Distribute hand-drawn maps from a National Weather Service Station. (Simply contact the office nearest you. See www.nws.org)

2. Review the information contained in the weather boxes from a previous lesson. Review the symbols in the weather boxes found on weather maps. Review the symbols for cold fronts and warm fronts. Remind students that the spurs or bubbles indicate the direction in which the front is moving. Encourage students to convert the temperatures and barometric pressures from the chart to the map on page 71. Demonstrate how to track isotherms from various cities; two distinct air masses should emerge. Students should draw a front symbol where they believe the two air masses meet.

- -

Exploration/Data Collection:

1. Record your best guesses about how meteorologists locate warm and cold air masses.

   _____

   _____

   _____

   _____

2. You are an expert weather forecaster for the Junior National Weather Service. Many calls from all over the Midwest have been received regarding the weather forecast. It is your responsibility to respond by reporting any fronts that may affect the weather and outdoor plans people may have. Examine the temperature data on the chart provided below. Draw a weather box around each city and transfer the data to its appropriate location on the weather map on page 71. Next, examine the map to determine *two* different types of air masses. Label the relative temperature of each air mass, e.g., warm or cold. Use colored pencils to represent where you believe a front exists. From what you recall about the pressure of air masses, label one air mass "low" and one air mass "high."

City	Temperature	City	Temperature
Chicago, IL	65°	Memphis, TN	85°
Cincinnati, OH	83°	Minneapolis, MN	60°
Des Moines, IA	65°	Nashville, TN	80°
Detroit, MI	79°	Oklahoma City, OK	69°
Little Rock, AR	68°	Springfield, IL	65°
Madison, WI	64°	St. Louis, MO	67°

Student Inquiry Activity **11** : Where the Action Is (cont.)

3. Determine whether the cold air mass is moving onto the area of warm air or vice versa. Explain how you know.

    _____

    _____

    _____

    _____

4. Along the border of the air masses on the map, draw a symbol for either the cold front or the warm front.

5. Predict what type of weather is likely to occur along the front you have just drawn.

    _____

    _____

    _____

    _____

Summary/What to Look For:
1. To what extent were students able to accurately identify cold and warm air masses using isotherms?
2. To what extent were students able to correctly label the front?
3. To what extent did students accurately infer the direction in which the front was moving?
4. To what extent were students able to infer the types of weather likely to occur along the front?
5. To what extent were students able to generate weather maps that accurately represented two air masses with a front?

Discussion Question/Assessment:
1. Create a weather map of your own. Create a data table for cities of your choice; be sure to include temperatures. Trade maps with a partner; the challenge is to use the data to identify the air masses and fronts. Describe the types of weather that are likely to occur along the front.

    _____

    _____

    _____

    _____

Name: _____ Date: _____

Student Inquiry Activity ⬛11 : Where the Action Is (cont.)

Weather Map

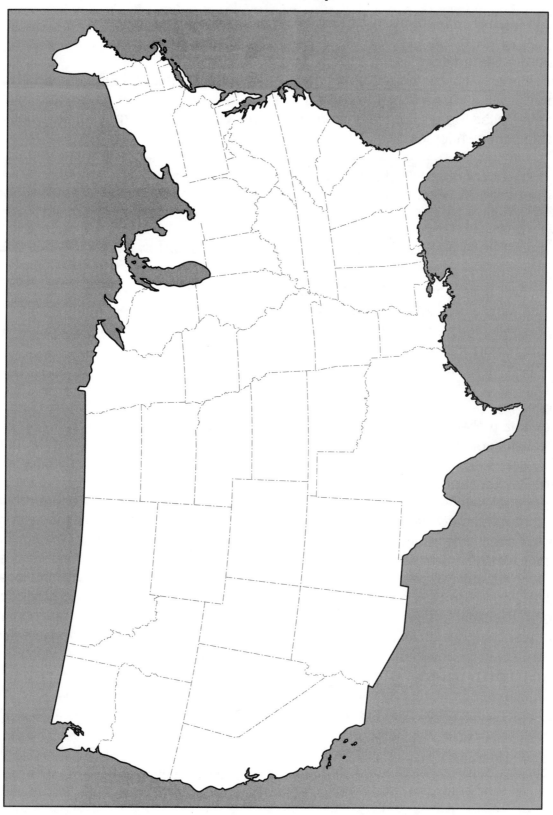

Name: _____ Date: _____

Student Inquiry Activity 12 : Mapping Your Way Through Weather

Topic: Weather—Weather Maps and Forecasting

Introductory Statement:

In this activity, you will apply the many ideas you have learned throughout the study of weather. You will gather and plot real-world weather data both from your town and from many cities in the United States. From this information, you will practice interpreting the weather data and create your own forecast.

NSES Content Standard E: Understanding About Science and Technology
Technology is essential to science, because it provides instruments and techniques that enable observation of objects and phenomena that are otherwise unobservable due to factors such as size, quantity, distance, location, and speed.

Science Skills and Concepts:

- Students will collect both local weather data and regional data via remote access.
- Students will plot and interpret weather data collected locally and via remote access.
- Students will infer weather systems and patterns based on weather maps created via local data and remote access.
- Students will evaluate the validity of remote data collection sites.

Materials:

Weather data (collected locally and via remote access)   Sticky notes
Large wall map of the United States   Science journals

Content Background/Procedures:

This activity can serve as a capstone event for the study of weather. It is an ongoing project that gives students cause to apply what they have learned in previous lessons. The application is real-time weather data collection, both locally, and via remote access (e.g., Internet, television, weather radio, etc). Students will each collect weather data from various cities individually, but they will pool and synthesize information to create forecasts for the local area. Predictions can then be tested by awaiting actual weather events. Errors in prediction may provide an excellent forum for troubleshooting and problem-solving in a very real context. The activity can be conducted for any duration; however, it is recommended to have the activity last several weeks. In this manner, students will be able to become more skilled at weather forecasting (e.g., learn from mistakes).

A local weather data collection station is needed, preferably near the classroom. Whereas in past lessons, local weather data was collected from several sites around the school grounds, it is recommended that one station be established and maintained as the "official weather station of the school and/or class." This will enhance the reliability of data collection, thereby enhancing the accuracy. Students must know that in order to make accurate forecasts, reliable data is needed. In that vein, they must collectively decide how weather data will be gathered

Name: _____ Date: _____

Student Inquiry Activity 12 : Mapping Your Way Through Weather (cont.)

systematically (e.g., source, time, manner, types, etc.). Discuss validity issues with remote data collection via the Internet. They may wish to select a consistent source of reliable data, such as The Weather Channel, The National Weather Service/NOAA, USA Today Weather, etc.

The local weather station should contain data collecting devices to fit what is known as a "weather box" for a site on a map (see example at right):

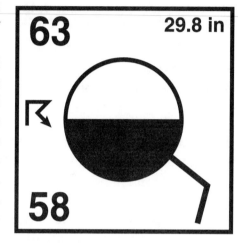

The local weather data collection station should contain a means by which to record temperature, barometric pressure, dew point, cloud types and percentage, wind speed and direction, and relative humidity. Based upon previous lessons, students should be familiar with each of the concepts; however, some review may be needed. Hold class meetings to determine decisions such as: frequency of data collection, order of people collecting data, how weekend data collection will occur, class-generated forms for systematic data collection, etc. Allow students to take ownership of the project; ideally, the teacher's role is to guide them and act in a support role as needed.

Students may need practice with weather boxes and maps prior to the actual data collecting and plotting. Refer to the skills learned in earlier lessons and point out that this activity will provide a chance to apply these skills.

In **Part I**, students will collect data locally at least two times per day and via remote access at least one time per day. The data should be systematically recorded in an area where all can see or have access. If possible, generate a large map of the United States, perhaps the size of a bulletin board and/or wall. Sticky notes provide an easy way to post data and still preserve the map. A written log should be kept to preserve the data as the map will change daily. Obviously, some geography skills will be needed; consider this as an excellent interdisciplinary opportunity.

Urge the students to select remote location sites that are convenient (accessible via the Internet) and relevant to your local weather conditions. For example, while it may be interesting to know the weather conditions in Hawaii, it will be of little use in forecasting weather in Dallas, Texas, for the next day. Instead, urge students to collect weather data, via remote access, for locations in which the local weather will be influenced within the next 24 to 48 hours. For example, if your classroom is in Cedar Rapids, Iowa, you may wish to choose locations such as Kansas City, Missouri; Omaha, Nebraska; and Des Moines, Iowa. In addition, it is suggested to select locations beyond where your local weather is likely to track. From Cedar Rapids, the weather might likely track easterly to cities such as Madison and Milwaukee, Wisconsin, or Chicago, Illinois. Sometimes weather systems track from northwest to southeast. In this case, students might consider cities like Peoria, Illinois, and Indianapolis, Indiana. In general, try to limit the remote locations to a 500-mile radius.

Name: _____ Date: _____

Student Inquiry Activity 12 : Mapping Your Way Through Weather (cont.)

Create teams (pairs) of data collectors for each location, both locally and via remote access. Depending upon the utility of the weather data in making forecasts, remote locations may need to be altered as the project unfolds. Otherwise, carefully select the remote locations and maintain a consistent data collection pattern. Naturally, data collection will probably take more time initially; students should become more efficient with practice. You may wish to have students practice collecting data for a period of time before actually using the data to generate forecasts (Part II); however, do not delay too long, or students may lose sight of the reason the data is being collected.

In **Part II**, students will begin generating simple 24- to 48-hour forecasts based on weather data collected via remote access. As students systematically collect and post data, a special emphasis should be placed on analysis. Repeatedly, pose the questions:

"So, what does this mean?"
"What sense can we make of the data?"
"What patterns do we see?"
"What conclusions can we draw?"

Answers to these questions will provide the basis for creating forecasts. Unless students learn how to use the weather data collected and posted, they will simply be good data collectors. Instead, we want them to be able to synthesize and analyze the data. Ultimately, we want them to evaluate their ability to interpret data and convert it into accurate weather forecasting. In reality, students will find out that this is much more difficult than it first appears. Encourage them not to become frustrated and give up. Some manner of quantifying margins of error may be desired. For example, students may predict a 24-hour high temperature of 68 degrees. If the high turns out to be 75, the margin of error assigned would be 7 degrees. Encourage students to maintain a record of the accuracy of their forecasts.

As appropriate, seize upon opportunities to reinforce cause/effect relationships commonly found in weather, e.g., strong cold fronts moving quickly into warm, moist air often result in strong storms and yield a variety of severe weather conditions. Naturally, this situation presents an opportunity to consider weather safety concepts. At times, weather patterns will be stable and yield little or no significant changes. This is a good reason to continue weather analysis over a period of time. If time and interest allow, a variety of weather patterns can be observed throughout the school year, including late summer, fall, winter, spring, and early summer.

After predicting and verifying weather forecasts for at least a week or so, consider inviting a meteorologist as a guest speaker. Encourage students to generate questions based upon the difficulties they have experienced. The idea is to bring in an expert as a consultant. Hopefully, students will find ways to fine-tune the process and become reenergized at the same time. Also, this will provide an excellent opportunity for the discussion of meteorology as a career. Encourage students to generate questions (in advance) regarding meteorology as a career.

Name: _____ Date: _____

Student Inquiry Activity 12 : Mapping Your Way Through Weather (cont.)

Another approach to studying weather forecasting involves students comparing their local real-time data to weather forecasts made by experts, prior to the day of data collection. For example, students might collect a daytime high temperature of 72 degrees. The actual

temperature (72 degrees) can then be compared to the forecasted high from the television meteorologist. In short, students are evaluating the accuracy of the television forecast, a day later. Even more interesting is to compare local real-time weather data to forecasts that originate from various mediums. For example, how does the accuracy of the forecasts of the television meteorologist compare to those of the National Weather Service? The Weather Channel? The radio station? The newspaper (local, regional, and national, e.g., *USA Today*)? Encourage students to speculate why some sources may be more accurate than others. For example, the people at the television station do not have nearly the same amount of time, equipment, and personnel as the National Weather Service. Ultimately, students can compare the accuracy of their own weather forecasts to the other mediums as well.

Assessment:

1. Throughout the entire project, take advantage of the opportunities to apply scientific inquiry along with the students. Have them record questions as they arise and collectively discuss ways to answer them. Is a testable hypothesis in order? Is reference work needed? Is the knowledge of an expert needed, and if so, in what ways can we access this? What new questions emerge as we try to answer our original questions?

2. Regular class meetings provide an opportunity to discuss what students have learned, still are learning, and want to learn about in the future. It is suggested for students to record minutes of the class meetings and provide opportunities for students to include their contributions to the project. Class meetings also provide a forum for ideas about what is working and what isn't, what needs to be changed and how, announcements, and general information sharing. As usual, allow students to take ownership of their learning during the class meetings.

Extension:

1. Some local television stations establish agreements with individuals and organizations to collect and report weather data on a regular basis. Often the television station management will provide basic weather data collection instruments. Contact your local media outlets for opportunities of this nature.

Extension Ideas and Interdisciplinary Applications

Weather & Geography & Industrial Technology:

Ask students to consider building codes, unique to geographical regions of the United States/world, which factor in weather conditions and phenomena. Some sample questions for investigation follow. Note the opportunities to cross the curriculum boundaries from the study of weather.

- What are building codes, and why are they necessary?
- In what ways do building codes vary from state to state?
- Who administers/regulates building codes?
- Identify weather conditions/phenomena that affect building codes (e.g., Florida and hurricanes).
- Specifically, in what ways is construction affected by weather phenomena? What industrial technology concepts are involved?

Farmer's Almanac:

Read the following excerpt from *The Handy Weather Answer Book* by Walter Lyons.

How Accurate is the Farmer's Almanac?

With respect to their weather forecasts, accuracy is not the almanacs' strong suit. However, the various almanacs published each year do have some good recipes for brownies and fudge. Their tide tables are dead on. The list of national holidays is handy. They also seem to have the astronomical predictions under control.

In 1504, Christopher Columbus was having trouble talking the natives of Jamaica into providing his crew with food and supplies. So, after consulting his early "almanac," he told natives if they did not cooperate, he would take the moon away. The lunar eclipse that followed greatly impressed the natives. p. 315

Lyons appears to believe that the Farmer's Almanac is not a reliable source of weather prediction. Do you agree? Why or why not? Support your claims.

Weather Lore:

Locate a resource entitled *Weather Proverbs: How 600 Proverbs and Poems Accurately Explain Our Weather* by George Freier.

What are your favorite weather sayings? Where did you learn of these sayings? How confident are you of their accuracy? Record several of your favorites and research to find their legitimacy! Share your findings with others.

National Sky Awareness Week:

Go online to **http://www.weatherworks.com/skyawareness.week.html**.

What is National Sky Awareness Week, and why is it important? In what ways can you become involved in this event?

Weather Poetry:

Locate and present weather related poems by the following authors/poets:

Robert Louis Stevenson - "wintertime"
Myra Cohn Livingston - "Coming Storm"
Seamus Heany - "Hailstones"
Robert Frost - "It Bids Pretty Fair" and "Atmosphere"
Christina G. Rossetti - "Who Has Seen the Wind?"
Carl Sandburg - "Fog"
Samuel Taylor Coleridge - "The Rime of the Ancient Mariner"

Try your hand at writing some weather poems of your own.

Wind Chill:

Recently, scientists have redefined the way in which **wind chill** is determined. What is wind chill, and how is it presently calculated? In what ways does this differ from how it was calculated in the past? Share your findings with others.

Effects of Weather on the Economy:

Various weather factors (extreme cold or heat, drought, excess rainfall, etc.) are likely to impact the economy indirectly. Consider one of the factors, such as extreme cold, and investigate its effects on the economy.

Consider various alternative forms of energy, e.g., wind, geothermal, solar, etc. Use the following questions as a guide to your research:

- What types of alternative forms of energy are available?
- In what ways does one's geographical location influence access to one or more of these energy sources?
- What are some of the pros/cons to alternative forms of energy?
- What environmental considerations are key to energy source decisions?
- If you were to build a new house, what forms of energy would you consider? Why?

Resource: **http://www.nrel.gov.wind/windfact.html**

Resources/Bibliography

WEATHER BOOK LIST:

Against The Elements Air, Jane Walker, Copper Beech Books, ISBN 0-7613-0855-5

And Now The Weather, Anita Ganeri, Aladdin Books, ISBN 0-689-71583-8

The Atmosphere, John Clark, Glouchester Press, ISBN 0-531-17367-4

Atmosphere, Climate, and Change, Scientific American Library, ISBN 0-7167-6028-2

Benjamin Franklin, Extraordinary Patriot, Deborah Kent, Scholastic, ISBN 0-590-46012-9

Blizzard, Dangerous Weather, Michael Allaby, Facts On File, ISBN 0-8160-3518-0

Blizzard, Disaster!, Dennis Brindell Fradin, Students' Press, ISBN 0-516-00857-9

Can It Really Rain Frogs?, Spencer Christian, John Wiley and Sons, ISBN 0-471-15290-0

Charlie Brown's 'Cyclopedia, VOL 9, Featuring: *The Earth, Weather, and Climate,* Funk and Wagnall, Inc., ISBN 0-394-84558-7

Clouds, Rain, and Snow, Dean Galiano, Rosen Publishing Co., ISBN 0-8239-3092-0

Clouds, Weather Report, Ann and Jim Merk, Rourke Corporation, ISBN 0-865993-389-8

Cloudy With a Chance of Meatballs, Judi Barrett, Houghton Mifflin Co., ISBN 0-395-45990-7

Disasters, Barbara Tufty, Dover, ISBN 0-486-25455-0

Do Tornadoes Really Twist?, Melvin and Gilda Berger, Scholastic Reference, ISBN 0-439-09584-0

Earth, Susanna Van Rose, Dorling Kindersley, ISBN 0-7894-5575-7

El Niño, Caroline Arnold, Clarion Books, ISBN 0-395-77602-3

Experiment With Weather, Miranda Bower, Lerner Publications, ISBN 0-8225-2458-9

Exploring the Sky by Day: The Equinox Guide to Weather and the Atmosphere, Terence Dickson, Fore Fly Books, ISBN 0-920656-71-4

Finding Out About Weather, Philip Carona, Benefic Press, 0-8175-7443-3

Flash, Crash, Rumble, and Roll, Franklin M. Branley, Harper Collins Publishers, ISBN 0-06-027859-5

The Handy Weather Answer Book, Walter Lyons, Visible Ink, ISBN 0-7876-1013-5

How the Weather Works, Michael Allaby, Reader's Digest, ISBN 0-89577-612-X

Hurricane and Tornado, Jack Challoner, Dorling Kindersley, ISBN 0-7894-6804-2

Hurricanes, Dean Galiano, Rosen Central, ISBN 0-8239-3095-5

Hurricanes, Victor Gentle, Gareth Stevens Publishing, ISBN 0-8368-2834-8

Hurricanes and Typhoons, Jacqueline Dineen, Gloucester Press, ISBN 0-531-17339-9

I Can Read About Weather, Robyn Supraner, Troll, ISBN 0-8167-4206-5

Magic Monsters Learn About Weather, Sylvia Root Tester, The Child's World, ISBN 0-89565-120-3

The Magic School Bus Inside a Hurricane, Joanna Cole, Scholastic ISBN 0-590-44687-8

Making and Using Your Own Weather Station, Beulah Tannenbaum, Franklin Watts, ISBN 0-531-10675-6

Mouse and Mole and the All-Weather Train Ride, Doug Cushman, Scholastic, ISBN 0-590-99692

National Audubon Society Field Guide To North American Weather, David Ludlum, Alfred A. Knopf, ISBN 0-679-40851-7

National Audubon Society First Field Guide: Weather, Jonathan Kahl, Scholastic, ISBN 0-590-05488-0

The Nature of and Science of Rain, Jane Burton and Kim Taylor, Gareth Stevens Publishing, ISBN 0-8368-1944-6

1001 Questions Answered About Hurricanes, Tornadoes and Other Natural Air Disasters, ISBN 0-486-25455-0 (Pbk)

Questions and Answers About Weather, Jean Craig, Scholastic ISBN 0-590-41142-X

Questions Kids Ask About Weather, Grolier Educational Corporation, ISBN 0-717-22559-3

Rain, Andres Llamas Ruiz, Sterling Publishing Co., ISBN 0-8069-9333-2

Skies Of Fury, Patricia and Thomas Svarney, Touchstone, ISBN 0-684-85000-1

Step by Step Weather, Paul Humphrey, Students' Press, ISBN 0-516-20238-3

Storms, Susan Canizares and Betsey Chessen, Scholastic, ISBN 0-590-10729-1

Storms: Facts, Stories, Activities, Jenny Wood, Scholastic, ISBN 0-590-93740-5

Storms, Weather Report, Ann and Jim Merk, Rourke Corporation, ISBN 0-865993-386-3

Thunderstorm!, Nathaniel Tripp, Dial Books, ISBN 0-8037-1365-7

Thunderstorms and Lightning, Dean Galiano, Rosen Central, ISBN 0-8239-3093-9

Tornado, Christopher Lampton, Milbrook Press, ISBN 1-56294-0032-5

Tornadoes, Jean Allen, Capstone Books, ISBN 0-7368-0588-5

Tornadoes, Ann Armbruster, Franklin Watts, ISBN 0-531-10755-8

Tornadoes, Dean Galiano, Rosen Publishing, 0-8239-3094-7

Tornadoes, Charles Rotter, Creative Education, ISBN 0-88682-712-4

Tornadoes, Seymour Simon, Morrow Junior Books, ISBN 0-688-14647-3

Tropical Storms and Hurricanes, Liza N. Burby, Rosen Publishing Group's, ISBN 0-8-239-5290-8

The Usborne Book of Weather Facts: Records, Lists, Facts, Comparisons, Anita Ganeri and Roger Hunt, Usborne, ISBN 0-860-20975-X

Wacky Weather, John Malam, Simon and Schuster, ISBN 0-689-81189-6

Wacky Weather, Annalisa McMorrow, Monday Morning, ISBN 1-57612-043-0

Watching Weather, Tom Murphee and Mary K. Miller, Henry Holt Books, ISBN 0-8050-4542-2

Weather, Martyn Bramwell, Franklin Watts, ISBN 0-531-14306-6 (2nd Edition)

Weather, Burroughs, Crowder, Robertson, Vallier-Talbot, Whitaker, Time-Life Books, ISBN 0-8094-9374-8

Weather, Pamela Chanko and Daniel Moreton, Scholastic, ISBN 0-590-10730-5

Weather, Brian Cosgrove, Dorling Kindersley, ISBN 0-7894-6577-9

Resources/Bibliography

Weather, Discovery Box, Scholastic, ISBN 0-590-92674-8

Weather, John Farndon, Dorling Kindersley, ISBN 0-7894-2985-3

Weather, Melissa Getzoff, Troll Associates, ISBN 0-8167-3608-1

Weather, Robin Kerrod, Gareth Stevens Publishing, ISBN 0-8368-2088-6

Weather, Sally Morgan, The Nature Company Discoveries Library, ISBN 0-8094-9370-5

Weather, Michael Oard, Master Books, ISBN 0-89051-211-6

Weather and Climate, David Flint, Gloucester Press, ISBN 0-531-17321-6

Weather and Climate, Alvin Silverstein, Virginia Silverstein, Laura Nunn, Twenty-first Century Books, ISBN 0-7613-3223-5

Weather and Climate, Barbara Taylor, Scholastic, ISBN 0-439-09962-5

Weather, An Explore Your World Handbook, Discovery Books, ISBN 1-56331-802-4

The Weather Book, Jack Williams, Vintage Books, ISBN 0-679-77665-6

Weather Everywhere, Denise Casey, Macmillian Books, ISBN 0-02-717777-7

Weather Facts, Philip Eden and Clint Twist, Dorling Kindersley, ISBN 0-7894-0218-1

Weather: Fun With Science, Steve Parker, Warwick Press, ISBN 0-531-19086-2

Weather Made Clear, Captain David C. Holmes, U.S.N., Sterling Publishing Co.

Weather: Make It Work!, Andrew Haslam and Barbara Taylor, World Book, ISBN 0-7166-5112-2

Weather Signs, Ann and Jim Merk, Rourke Corporation, ISBN 0-86593-388-X

The Weather Sky, Bruce McMillan, Farrar Straus Giroux, ISBN 0-374-38261-1

Weather Station, Activity Fun Pack, Funfax Book, ISBN 0-7894-3006-1

Whatever the Weather, Karen Wallace, Dorling Kindersley, ISBN 0-7894-4750-9

What Will the Weather Be?, Julian May, Creative Educational Society, ISBN 0-871-91063-2

What Will the Weather Be Like Today?, Paul Rogers, Scholastic, and ISBN 0-590-45013-1

Wild, Wet and Windy—The Weather, Claire Llewellyn, Candlewick Press, ISBN 0-7636-0340-X

The Wind, Jeanne Bendick, Rand McNally and Co.

Wind, Susan Canizares and Betsey Chessen, Scholastic, ISBN 0-590-10726-7

Wind, Francesca Grazzini, Kane/Miller Book Publishers, ISBN 0-916291-67-7

Wind and Weather, Scholastic, ISBN 0-590-47646-7

Wind and Weather, Barbara Taylor, Franklin Watts, ISBN 0-531-14184-5

Wind and Weather, Time-Life Books, ISBN 0-8094-4829-7

Winter Weather, John Mason, Bookwright Press, ISBN 0-531-18358-0

WEATHER CURRICULUM MATERIALS:

BSCS Science T.R.A.C.S. Series

    Investigating Weather, 2, Teacher's Edition, ISBN 0-7872-2280

    Investigating Weather Systems, 5, Teacher's Edition, ISBN 0-7872-2288-7

    Investigating Weather Systems, 5, ISBN 0-7872-2268-2

DSM II Series, Delta Education, Teacher's Guides

    Amazing Air, 2-3, ISBN O-87504-230-9

    Weather Instruments, 3-5, ISBN 0-87504-186-8

    Solar Energy, 5-6, ISBN 0-87504-111-6

    Weather Forecasting, 5-6, ISBN 0-87504-123-X

Overhead and Underfoot, 3-5, AIMS Education Foundation, Revised Edition, ISBN 1-881431-52-5

Project Atmosphere, American Meteorological Society

    Clouds

    Hazardous Weather

    Jet Streams

    Water Vapor and the Water Cycle

    Today's Weather

    Weather Satellites

Project Earth Science: Meteorology (2nd Edition). 2001. National Science Teachers Association. Arlington, VA. ISBN 0-8735-5123-0

Project SafeSide, On The SafeSide With The Weather Channel

Wild About Weather, National Wildlife Federation, Learning Triangle Press, ISBN 0-07-047098-7

RECOMMENDED SOFTWARE:

The Weather Channel's Everything Weather by Sunburst Technology

Science Court: Seasons and *Water Cycle* by Tom Snyder Productions

Teacher's Guide For Winds, Riverside Scientific, Inc.

WW2010, the Weather World 2010 Project, Hybrid Multimedia Educational CD-ROM, 2nd Edition, Department of Atmospheric Sciences, University of Illinois at Champaign-Urbana

RECOMMENDED WEBSITES:

www.education.noaa.gov

www.usatoday.com

www.weather.com

www.weatherworks.com

www.weatherandthensome.com

www.weatherdesk.org

COMPLETE WEATHER-RELATED RESOURCE LIST:

For an exhaustive listing of weather-related resources, consult "Resource Listing for Weather and Climate Instruction" by Edward J. Hopkins, University of Wisconsin, Madison. A pdf download is available at http://www.nssl.noaa.gov/resources

BIBLIOGRAPHY/REFERENCE:

Brunet, C., Holle, R., Mogil, H., Moran, J., Phillips, D. (1999). *Weather.* New York: Discovery Books.

Burroughs, W., Crowder, B., Robertson, T., Vallier-Talbot, E., Whitaker, R. (1996). *Weather.* Sydney: Time-Life Books.

Eden, P., Twist, C. (1995). *Weather Facts.* New York: Dorling Kindersley.

Graedel, T., Crutzen, P. (1995). *Atmosphere, Climate, and Change.* New York: Scientific American Library.

Murphee, T., Miller, M.K. (1998). *Weather Watching: A Low Pressure Book About High Pressure Systems and Other Weather Phenomena.* New York: Henry Holt and Company.

Sager, R., Ramsey, W., Phillips, C., Watenpugh, F. (2002). *Modern Earth Science.* Austin: Holt, Rinehart and Winston.

Williams, J. (1997). *The Weather Book.* New York: Vintage Books.